THE 4 STREAMS OF LEADERSHIP

Transform Yourself Into an Overachiever Manager

DALMO CIRNE

PEAKPOINT
—— PRESS ——

Peakpoint Press books may be purchased in bulk at special discounts for sales promotion, corporate gifts, fund-raising, or educational purposes. Special editions can also be created to specifications. For details, contact the Special Sales Department, Skyhorse Publishing, 307 West 36th Street, 11th Floor, New York, NY 10018 or info@skyhorsepublishing.com.

Peakpoint® and Peakpoint Press® are registered trademarks of Skyhorse Publishing, Inc.®, a Delaware corporation.

Visit our website at www.skyhorsepublishing.com.

10 9 8 7 6 5 4 3 2 1

Library of Congress Cataloging-in-Publication Data is available on file.

Cover design by David Ter-Avanesyan

ISBN: 978-1-5107-8518-2
Ebook ISBN: 978-1-5107-8663-9

Printed in the United States of America

To the two people who have taught me the most: my kids, Adam and Bianca.

And to my wife, Renata, who transformed my world forever.

Contents

Introduction

November 11, 2013, was day one at a fledgling startup in New York City. I was a bit apprehensive since this was the first time I was expected to build and lead a team, and there were no corporate instructions or a pre-existing rule book for me to use as a safety net to guide me through the process. Had I reached the position in which incompetence was bestowed upon me? Was the Peter Principle right?

The first twenty years of my professional career were dedicated to being an individual contributor (IC), working as a hands-on software engineer, from the RiskMetrics Group to Disney. I had the opportunity to help design and build products in a range of industries, from finance and management to entertainment. But I had reached a point in my career where the challenges before me were too big for any given individual to tackle within a reasonable time frame. Here I am talking about leading entire teams and projects, not the usual collaborative teamwork that happens when working together on a product.

In the beginning, everything felt complicated since I lacked the knowledge to manage a team or project, peers, upper management, or even myself. As a manager, my skills in software architecture, programming languages, and technology in general were important but less relevant. I realized that I needed to learn a new discipline, but no company provided adequate training to help me make the transition. That fell to me, so I read voraciously about management, struggling to piece together a workable path forward. It wasn't easy.

I learned from friends and colleagues at other companies that I wasn't alone. My journey to becoming an effective manager helped me realize that I wasn't isolated in thinking there is a paucity of skilled managers and people leaders, particularly at technology companies, so much so that I came to view this as something of a management crisis. As one who is always looking for a better way, I devised my own method for engaging and motivating my teams to create and follow through so successfully that I was swamped with requests to share my "secret."

The story of how I developed *The 4 Streams of Leadership* (T4SOL, or (/'tæsol/) phonetically) is filled with setbacks and advances. It began in 2013 when I joined mParticle, then a young, bare-bones startup. I was one of the first people to come on board, and we were on a mission. My title was senior director of engineering, but in the early days, there were really no people to manage. That would come later. My job was to develop the architecture and implement the mobile component of the platform. Having come from Disney with a strong technical background and a great track record of building and deploying products, I was a perfect match for the job.

We were building new things, testing the limits of the technology. There were days when I thought it would be impossible to come up with answers to the challenges we had encountered, but somehow, we always ended up finding our way to a solution. The company was growing fast, and I played a significant role in taking mParticle from zero to one—a phrase popularized by tech entrepreneur Peter Thiel.

However, with rapid growth, new challenges emerged, and they were much bigger than any one person could tackle. We needed to grow the team. That is when I started to fall short of expectations. I was great at my job as an engineer and had had some minor managerial experience, but I had yet to master what it meant to be a great manager. My "senior director" title said one thing, while my lack of in-depth management knowledge said another. The result? New members of the team lacked purpose, the features of the same software product implemented on different hardware platforms were not cohesive, and the team's priorities were generally misaligned.

At that moment, I realized I needed to reinvent myself and learn a new set of skills, so I embarked upon a quest to discover what it means to be a manager. In my mind, I understood that I needed to press the reset button and start a new career nearly from scratch. It was a moment of humility and acknowledgment that I was back to being the student.

I needed to learn all there was about management, absorbing content like a sponge absorbs water. I read many of the classics plus several more recent books and articles on leadership and management, and I exchanged notes and sought advice from various acquaintances, colleagues, and friends who are managers themselves. I was devouring everything I could get my hands on. Most importantly, I put my new knowledge into practice. I experimented as I went, learning from conjectures and refutations, trial and error, empirically verifying or disproving what works and what doesn't.

I left mParticle in 2017 with an amicable relationship. It was the right thing for me to do; I had learned an enormous amount while there and knew I had to keep learning even more to become the manager I believed I could be.

My next job was at the startup Clarifai. It was a place to start fresh and an opportunity to practice all that I had been learning. I was determined to become the best manager in the company. My title was director of engineering. Although on the surface it may have looked like a demotion, I didn't care. I was grateful for the opportunity.

The story at Clarifai was a much happier one. There, I built a team of A players. We all liked working together, and we learned a lot from each other. For the first time, I felt I was becoming a good manager, and there was evidence to corroborate that: the practices we put in place started being referred to as an "exemplary" model for other teams. The team grew, my responsibilities grew, and soon the scope of my job expanded to managing engineering on multiple projects, including the most important project in the company with the US Department of Defense.

The seeds of what would soon become this book were germinating. I understood my strengths and where to apply them, and my limitations and when to invest in improving them. Underpinning my success at Clarifai were a few important realizations: Strategy and communication must flow in all directions; managing your direct reports is only part of the equation; it is necessary to cultivate a relationship with stakeholders and peers then manage each relationship, each in its appropriate way. After studying, practicing, and gathering feedback, I started to see a pattern forming. At a certain moment, I had an epiphany, and a light bulb flashed on. The concept of *The 4 Streams of Leadership* was born.

In early 2020, roughly at the beginning of the COVID-19 pandemic, I accepted a job offer from Workday. My family and I moved from New York to Colorado; it was a leap of faith in the company and a bet on the future. I took all that I had developed with me and was committed to continue building on it.

This new chapter felt like the perfect opportunity to apply the practices described in *The 4 Streams of Leadership* at a larger corporation. I joined Workday to manage machine learning engineering applied to financials. Initially, I managed the product Journal Insights, then added more products to my responsibilities, including Customer Payment Matching, and Expense Protect. Later I got the Financial Planning and Analysis team transferred under my supervision and proceeded to pivot from a project that was struggling to one that was building a successful large language model (LLM) product. There were four different teams, four different projects, and four successful products. As I took on more responsibilities, managing other managers became part of the job. These managers inherited some of the projects I had overseen and are doing a fantastic job using the tools, processes, and operational models presented in this book.

With management success under my belt, friends and colleagues started asking me for advice regarding how to handle certain situations and what approach to take in certain scenarios. I am happy to say that my advice helped them all.

That advice has become this book, and it will be different than what you have heard or read before. Most management books focus on one stream, and more often than not that stream is *downstream*. In other words, they focus directly on the people and tasks for which they are responsible. But effective managers are also adept at managing three other streams: upstream, sidestream, and—core to it all—the reservoir. This book addresses the *why*, *what*, *when*, and *how* of management. And it is one of the easiest management books to implement.

Management is a craft that requires many skills: technical, emotional, hierarchical, and beyond. Managers become less effective when they mainly harness the raw power of just one area, when they focus on delivering deliverables as the primary decision driver, or when they act with good intentions but are unaware of system complexities. Then, the team, the project, and the company suffer ailments such as low team morale, poor product quality, and bad reputation for the firm.

Great management requires filling the knowledge gap that all leaders have, both seasoned managers and individual contributors transitioning to management. The dual mission of this book is to be a source of learning and a reference guide to make all managers more enabled and effective. In these pages you will find foundational frameworks, operational models, teaching tools, practical examples, clear explanations, and knowledge that can transform almost anyone into a great manager.

I teach and employ the unique concept of leadership streams to represent the flow of activities associated with management. I group those activities into four distinct categories to make it easier to understand and implement them. Each stream requires special knowledge and skill. By learning and applying the content presented here, you will become a better manager and avoid common misconceptions and mistakes.

Companies of all sizes, including large companies with training programs, struggle to produce skilled or even competent managers, making it harder to promote organically from within, thus skewing the selection to outside candidates. A better approach would be to create a balance of outsiders (who bring fresh ideas and new practices) and insiders (with domain knowledge and rapport with the team). As you read this book, you will be able to immediately apply what you have learned at your job.

The lessons and operational frameworks you will read on these pages can be applied in an age of rapid technological change, artificial intelligence, and distributed teams with employees on the same team working in various locations.

If you feel disconnected or have negativity toward your role as a manager, that is normal, especially when you are unprepared. Think of the journey as navigating the rapids of a river with turbulent emotions. As you experiment and evolve from one identity to another, you will likely feel the loss of familiar things such as:

- **Identity.** You used to be an expert; now you are navigating uncharted waters.

- **Turf.** You oversaw technology; you were creating things.
- **Control and structure.** The decisions were familiar; you knew what to do and what the plan was.
- **Attachments** to colleagues, hierarchy, team dynamics.
- **Meaning.** You felt fulfilled at your previous job; you were completing assignments, making progress.

How you respond to these changes will determine your success. Don't get stuck in nostalgia. Together we are going to sink your old ship, craft a new one, and sail toward brighter days. Start to feel excited about the possibilities and consider marking this rite of passage with a celebration that you design to clearly delineate your past from your inspiring future.

I believe the map you were following on that previous voyage was leading you astray. That's the key reason I wrote this book: because most books about management are nearly impossible to put into practice. The authors tell stories, real or fictional, that are analogies, metaphors, or anecdotes related to points they are trying to make. Although well meaning, they fail to understand that prior knowledge of the subject matter is necessary to understand the key point being communicated in the story. And without prior knowledge, this becomes a chicken-and-egg problem: one cannot understand the moral of the story without existing domain knowledge, and the same person cannot gain domain knowledge without understanding the story.

Those books may illustrate a subject, but seeing any similarity between these tales and real life requires that readers have existing knowledge of the subjects. Take away the stories and those books become much shorter. I deliberately avoided such tales and analogies in this book because they carry only opinion and guesswork. With just those, a reader will find it difficult to translate the moral of stories to their own domains.

Yes, their words may be compelling and make sense to readers. We want to believe in their idealized visions. However, when trying to put all those "lessons" into practice, we hit a wall of inevitable frustration amid the thought "I may not be good enough for the job." What is proposed is that you become a romanticized quintessential manager. And if you are not able to be that person and cannot make the nearly impossible happen, it is your fault. Why? Because you did not follow all the minute details of their recipe precisely.

Authors propose and ask for almost superhuman discipline and adherence to ideal processes that are not sustainable in the long run by most professionals. The authors give advice and propose habits, routines, and mental models, many of which they themselves either cannot or do not follow.

This book adopts a different approach. It presents explanatory knowledge for why to manage, what to manage, when to manage, and how to do the management of the *why*, *what*, and *when*. In addition to the theoretical content in each chapter, whenever possible, I complement the explanations with real-life examples to illustrate a concept or to further understanding. Many people learn better when absorbing information mimetically and replicating it themselves, adapting the case to their own circumstances.

Here I share the result of thousands of hours of trial-and-error experimentation, insights, theories, discoveries, operational frameworks, and the distilled compilation of verifiable practices that I am convinced will be particularly useful in helping you become a successful manager.

Each segment of this book represents a domain or a subdomain of the leadership streams, presenting material and lessons that are specific to that area. Chapters and sections are organized in such a way that, in most cases, you don't have to know about the previous ones. I recommend to first read it from cover to cover. After that, use the table of contents or the index to jump to topics or keywords of interest.

Most of the examples shown here—given that so much of my career has been spent in software engineering—will be related to software products and services. I trust that you will be able to easily draw parallels to instances in your field, even if you are in a field unrelated to technology; you will see that the underlying lessons and techniques are universal.

The framework I use begins, as I have said, with identifying management as four main streams that need to be managed independently yet together, and all in harmony. This construct is the essence of my system of the four streams of leadership. These four streams will be our "compass rose," such that instead of being oriented by the cardinal directions, they will help us navigate the job and the creative craft of management.

Throughout the book, we will rely on both quantitative and empirical frameworks to help us explore the details, intricacies, and expectations from each of the streams.

My sincere hope is that many journeys arise from these pages. May they help you write the next chapter of your own story. You will need to implement the concepts as practice and make your own mistakes. Here, you will find the tools, instruments, and maps to do that. They will help you navigate the waters of your own journey. You will be confident that you know what needs to be done and how to do it.

By no stretch of the imagination are the contents here immutable and static. Nor will you find dogmatic truths. On the contrary, everything in this book is expressed in a neutral, nonjudgmental manner and will evolve as companies, people, technologies, teams, and managers change. Future editions will continue to adhere to the highest standards of authoritative research and information.

The timeless principles in this book will work for you whether you apply them to companies where teams collaborate and create on-site or with distributed teams. Remote work, though not a recent phenomenon, has become a worldwide reality for many businesses as a result of the COVID-19 lockdowns. Many companies have discovered that they can continue to operate completely remotely or in a hybrid mode. Other companies, due to the nature of the products and services they offer, need their teams to work in an office. Whichever the case, the teachings and techniques contained here are applicable to all those scenarios. The lessons you will learn here will make management a second-nature skill, innate as part of the air you breathe.

In writing the chapters ahead, I imagine primarily addressing a few groups of readers: professionals transitioning into management; new managers who feel they need training; established managers who want to update or expand their knowledge of tools, processes, and principles; companies that want to invest in upskilling managers to reach higher levels of performance; and students with management aspirations.

Keep the book easily accessible and use it as reference material for practices you haven't yet incorporated, situations that happen infrequently, or when you need to review a particular topic.

It is time to set sail on your new or expanded career in management. Embrace the change. To begin, there are several responsibilities and tasks you need to take care of to make your team, your project, and your company successful. Let's get started.

CHAPTER 1

The 4 Streams of Leadership (T4SOL)

Learn from the mistakes of others. You can't live long enough to make them all yourself.

—Eleanor Roosevelt

We will begin by asking a question: Why does any company need to hire a manager? Answering it requires us to know what value managers add to products and services. Finding the response to this and other related questions is essential to the journey you will take as a manager. In this book, I will talk about what a manager does and the objectives that drive management. To do this, I will focus on how to deliver sustainable results that work well in the long run and how to know what to do when faced with the omnipresent demands of the four leadership streams.

There is a popular proverb that says no one lives long enough to learn everything from scratch. Before you embark on a personal voyage to find the undiscovered answers yourself, stop for a moment and consider learning from other people's lessons and mistakes. Then make some of your own.

Management is a creative craft; it is not art. Art does not require objective criteria for evaluation; management does. Management is measured by its effectiveness, then its efficiency. Although the performance of most people using the same tools is similar, there are those extraordinary individuals who execute dramatically better than most.

A manager often has technical knowledge but should avoid being a technical leader—unless dictated by circumstances. As a manager, you are a facilitator, catalyst, and multiplier for a team to do its best work.

Rather than attempting to be a technician by providing suggestions for ways to do things, present the problem and ask for solutions. For example: We need to implement feature X. What do you recommend? How will you implement this?

Wait for and listen to the answers. When appropriate, provide critical feedback. Be mindful of the gap between reaction and response (more about that in "Behavior" in chapter 2).

Basic principles of accounting tell us that if an item costs more than the value it produces, the investment is not worthwhile. Using this reasoning, the corollary for the value managers bring to teams and products must be the following: conceiving, implementing, and delivering would be more expensive compared to not having managers.

Exploring this thought further, let's begin by asking ourselves the following question related to, for example, the field of engineering: could engineers self-govern themselves in projects other than hobbies or small-scale production? Yes, theoretically, they could. They have self-managing abilities; they are smart people. This, however, begs a follow-up question: is this the best way to deploy engineering resources? Would having engineers multitasking between technical and managerial work yield the best returns?

Rather than focusing on technical activities, engineers would divert effort and attention from where their education, talent, and experience are strongest to work on managerial activities. Asking them to perform additional tasks outside their area of expertise will lead to some of them protesting that "this is not part of the job description." They may not want to take part in those activities, nor would they be technically prepared to do so.

The contrasts between the two dynamics would evolve to most engineers choosing to focus on technical work, whereas a few of them would dedicate their attention to managerial tasks, bringing the discussion full circle to the place where it started. Projects are complex systems and require specializing in either technical or managerial responsibilities.

Perverse incentives are also a factor in self-governing bodies. Take for instance a senior engineer assigning easier tasks to themselves and relegating more difficult ones to junior engineers, thus giving the perception to outside observers that those senior engineers are more productive and as a result, they might demand higher compensation. A concomitant side effect could be that junior engineers are perceived as less productive, thus undermining their prospects for career growth, which could lead them to search for better opportunities elsewhere. All the while, the product would see little to no progress. The fate of the project would be the first casualty.

Here is yet another scenario under self-governance: analysis paralysis when significant changes are necessary. Negotiations about what to change and when to engage would be inefficient, requiring almost unanimous consensus on every decision. With any objection, the discussion could drag on and on, gravely compromising productivity.

What Is Management?

Generally speaking, management is hierarchical because that is a necessary condition for arbitrating decisions. However, it comes with the mission and the responsibility of executing first, effectively, and second, efficiently. We will explore this topic further in the section on "Effectiveness and Efficiency" in chapter 5).

Think about an event where a system malfunction is affecting customers. A manager becomes essential in coordinating the implementation of the solution. Without a central, accountable figure, it is distinctly possible that the situation would spiral out of control, with teams pointing fingers at each other to avoid being held accountable. Meanwhile, the desired outcome from all parties concerned is finding a solution to the problem. A manager can centralize responsibility without necessarily attributing blame to teams.

This leads us to conclude that the primary roles of management are to be effective in executing solutions, to deliver them efficiently within a reasonable amount of time, and to determine how to allocate resources optimally.

The job of a manager extends beyond managing a team. Great managers must manage themselves, the project, and operations. They must cultivate relationships with cross-functional peers and make sure different teams are collaborating. But it doesn't stop here.

Your relationship with your peer product manager is strategic and must be a good one. You are both working toward the same objective. I say that because the needs and incentives of the product and engineering departments may not always be aligned, thus creating friction in, for instance, features, scope, and timelines. You both must be honest in your conversations and speak what needs to be spoken. A healthy and collaborative partnership between the product and engineering departments is a prerequisite for the success of a project.

Let's look at the other essential groups that need managing. These include upper management, stakeholders, and customers. It is important to be a good communicator and a good writer to report on the status of the project, speak about road maps, present the details of the plan and its execution, and manage expectations.

Most importantly, you need to manage yourself. That involves self-awareness of your strengths and your weaknesses. Be aware of the subjects where you are strong, the places where your contributions add the most value, and the areas where you will need help from your team, your peers, or someone else.

When you are new to management, various routines start forming. People will reach out for answers, meeting invites will proliferate, and the world will feel quite different. Your initial reaction may be to rebel, but rather than fighting it, embrace it. Those are the new tools you have at your disposal to do your job. Remember, now you are playing a different game in which the old rules no longer apply. You will need to adapt to those changes.

At the end of the day, you will be leading a project and a group of people to execute on a vision. Use your best judgment to help your team, project, and company.

The Foundational Four

A perennial river is characterized by an uninterrupted stream that continuously delivers water, irrespective of the season. Analogous to a perennial river, management is an activity that experiences a constant flow of tasks that repeatedly demand attention, supervision, communication, and so forth. Rather than stressing out about the volume and velocity of the streams, it is better to remain as calm as most parts of a river, accepting that there will also be moments of rapids and turbulence. This book presents the knowledge, explanations, and tools you will need to navigate those waters successfully—especially useful in today's climate of accelerated technological advancements and AI developments.

This is the thinking behind a new leadership concept I call "The 4 Streams of Leadership." It defines the plurality of streams where managerial time and effort should be focused, shines a light on what managers do—or are expected to do—and allows for a clearer understanding and perception of the value managers add to the team and the company.

Management is a cross-disciplinary activity that sits at the intersection of four foundational streams that we must manage: reservoir, downstream, upstream, and sidestream.

Those are the *what, why, when,* and *how* of essential management. You can see each stream represented in Figure 1.1. We will explore each of them in depth in the chapters to come.

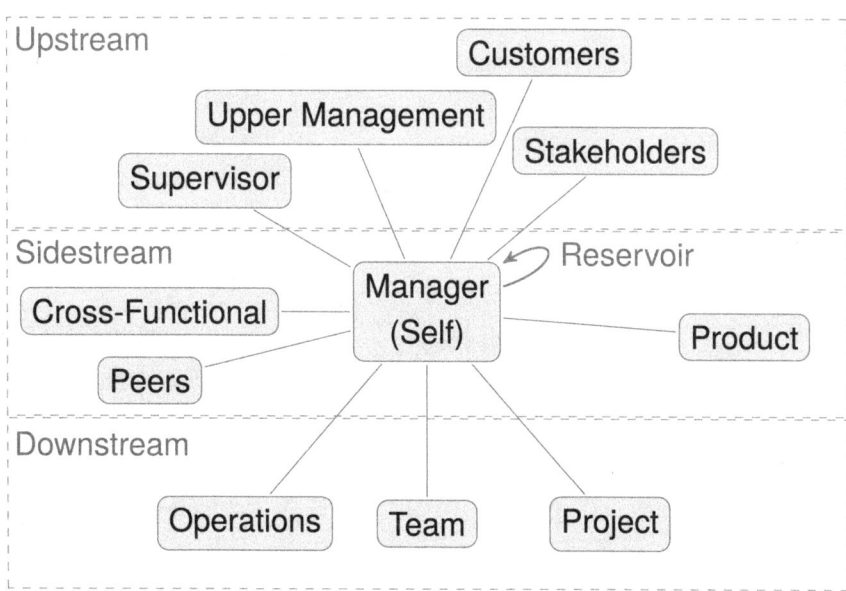

Figure 1.1: The 4 Streams of Leadership: Reservoir, Downstream, Upstream, and Sidestream.

The journey begins with managing the reservoir, which means, of course, managing yourself. Introspection can be incredibly difficult because it is necessary to face yourself and become aware of your strengths and weaknesses. Then, identify the core values that will form the foundation for you and the team; those are superior in every way to perks, which are secondary. Be ruthless about controlling the time on your calendar, be rational making decisions, and be trusting delegating.

Next, learn how to manage downstream, which involves managing the team, projects, and operations. This includes hiring and assembling the team to work together, establishing a sustainable productivity velocity, helping with career growth, providing the circumstances for quality of life, prioritizing work, being effective, setting up routines, and insisting on and measuring quality—all while having fun.

Upstream management means working with upper management (including your immediate supervisor), stakeholders, and customers. This could involve deciding whether to invest in a product, finding alignment, getting proposals approved, monitoring performance indicators, establishing goals, delivering presentations, and working with customers.

Managing sidestream is the fourth and final stream. Its focus is on collaborating with your counterparts, such as the product team and cross-functional peers. Your collective goal is to find the best market fit for your product.

The system of leadership streams is far from being a panacea framework. Instead, it symbolizes and acknowledges that each stream requires different sets of skills and styles that are necessary for being successful as a manager and people leader.

The Why, What, When, and How

Alignment magnifies the time and effort put into building a product or service, and perhaps the best way I know to bring people into alignment is to communicate *why* something will be done. Even if some may disagree with you, they will, at least, be able to commit since there is understanding.

It is your responsibility, the responsibility of the product manager, your manager, stakeholders, and your team to define *what* to do. Be expansive when inviting people to the conversation and considering their opinions and suggestions. However, you are not required to incorporate them. At the end of the day the buck stops with you. (You are not managing by consensus.)

Timing is everything. It is vital to understand *when* to set core values, hire a new person, delegate a task, host a retrospective, communicate with stakeholders, and so forth. If done too early, the effort could have been applied elsewhere with better returns. If done too late, the opportunity may have passed, or the damage may have been done.

Combined, the *why*, *what*, and *when* can only take you so far. Without knowing *how* to do the *what* and *when*, you are left in the realm of ideas and possibilities, unable to make it concrete. Without the *how*, somebody else will come and eat your lunch.

Each of these words will not appear explicitly in explanations and frameworks. Instead, what you will see are explanatory knowledge, definitions, timing, and practical examples.

For instance, processes (the *what*) are usually established in order to reliably reproduce outcomes (the *why*) when the scale of operations reach a certain threshold (the *when*). The associated procedures often take the form of a workflow—imagine a flowchart in which itemization of tasks, approvals, definition of roles, and so on are necessary (the *how*).

CHAPTER 2

Managing the Reservoir

Masters in the art of living draw no sharp distinction between their work and their play, their labor and their leisure, their mind and their body, their education and their recreation. They hardly know which is which. They simply pursue their vision of excellence through whatever they are doing and leave others to determine whether they are working or playing. To themselves, they always appear to be doing both.

—Lawrence Pearsall Jacks

Managing yourself is among the hardest things you will ever do. Mastering it is a requisite for becoming effective at managing a team and a project. There is a natural operating system inside you that determines how you behave and respond to different situations. Analogous to a computer operating system, you can learn more about it, install programs, and perform upgrades.

Managing the reservoir means, among other things, that you need to be aware of the requirements of your job and how to do it. It also means that you need to delegate competently without abdicating your responsibilities, manage your time, and use your actions as leverage for having a positive impact on the team's output.

These things are easier said than done. The inner journey begins by becoming aware of what you need to manage in yourself before you can improve over time. There will be moments when you feel alone, isolated without answers, and not able to share your thoughts with the team.

You may end up coping with feelings of instability and being out of place. Try to develop (if one doesn't already exist) a group of peer managers, find a mentor, or talk to colleagues you can trust. These relationships will help you get through the tough times and the moments of doubt. Just as with Alexandre Dumas's memorable Three Musketeers motto ("One for all, all for one"), be there for them the same way they are there for you. Speak and listen, take and offer advice, and accept and give help. Give back as much as you receive, if not more. This way, everyone will grow stronger together.

Unlike the other streams, whose flow is intuitive to understand, a reservoir evokes stillness rather than movement. Effective management will require discipline and vigilance in your behavior and self-awareness in maintaining your values while growing steadily as a manager. That is how your reservoir will remain full and enable success in all other, outward streams.

Self-Awareness

Becoming self-aware, in this context, means reflecting on yourself and identifying which areas are your strengths and which areas are your weaknesses. This is a difficult task and requires absolute honesty with oneself. You are embarking on a journey of self-discovery; you are not trying to impress others. Do yourself a favor and be candid; resist evaluating yourself in any way that makes not being self-aware more acceptable.

Why did you become a manager? Consider the following questions to understand or accept why you want to become a manager or want to continue to be one:

- Is it because of the salary? Many senior individual contributors are compensated better than managers.
- Do you like dealing with people? Do you like listening and challenging them to become better versions of themselves?

- The best teams have people who can debate ideas effectively. Are you comfortable having your positions questioned, and can you change your opinion in light of new information?
- Can you step away from the spotlight and give credit to the team and to peers?
- Are you happy being among people who are subject matter experts?
- Have you had a position of leadership before (technical or otherwise)? Do you need to learn and build better leadership skills?
- If you are not enjoying your management role, should you consider giving it up?

Self-awareness will arrive accompanied by choice and responsibility; that is, you will have the choice to play to your strengths and the responsibility to do so. Sharing your awareness of strengths and weaknesses with the whole world is not required. You do, however, need to be honest with yourself. This is key to becoming a better manager.

Knowledge of your strengths will allow for more effective meetings, discussions, planning, decision-making, and interactions with your team. Knowing your weaknesses will allow you to act and seek advice from other people, such as team members, peers, mentors, and other respected counselors.

Contrary to intuition, seeking advice about your weaknesses is a sign of strength. It means that you are open to knowledgeable feedback and criticism and support acting on what matters, which means addressing the situation at hand and getting better outcomes. When talking with others, begin with sharing a question or a situation with them and then asking for their opinion regarding how they would address it.

Listen attentively to what is said, and keep an open mind—free of biases about different perspectives. Use your judgment regarding the advice received, and consider whether it should influence your next steps. The decision on the course of action is yours, but by talking to others, you put yourself in a position where you must perceive circumstances differently. As a result, you are better prepared.

Corporate communication and business literature often hold up self-lessness as an eternal virtue. The idea is to encourage people to suppress their egos and aspire to become selfless as a career goal. I dispute this principle. The way I see it, the response to an inflated ego is self-aware-ness, openness to being coached, and the intrinsic desire to continuously improve, rather than to become selfless.

Asking an individual, a team, or a body of employees to be selfless is to deny people's humanity. Creativity, innovation, explanations, and more come from the self. Execution requires the combined effort of many. Products are only possible and can only be successful with the collective collaboration of all the people on the team. Ideas, suggestions, initiatives, and so forth are integral parts of the self.

Over the course of your career, you may encounter toxic colleagues or leaders who do not exhibit self-awareness or productive collaboration. How do you manage them? Even some of the most vaunted businesspeo-ple have said that if such employees are very disruptive, consider manag-ing them right out of the company. If that is not possible, find a better job and leave the company yourself.

Behavior

Whether water enters or leaves a reservoir, it is checked for cleanliness and tested for pollutants. The same principles apply to how you behave as a leader.

The people with whom you interact will be evaluating your reputa-tion every day—every time you speak, decide, give feedback, or react to a crisis. These are but a few examples of how you are constantly under a microscope.

Although it is true that you do not have to live up to everything that others expect of you, when someone is in a position of leadership, some behaviors are necessary while other behaviors should be avoided.

One skill a manager, or any leader, must learn is the ability to own the gap between reaction and response. Hearing about good news, being told about a critical bug in the system, participating in a technical dis-cussion—all of these will affect your emotions, inciting joy, anger, excite-ment, and more. That said, it is essential to understand the gap between reaction (internal) and response (external).

Consider the case of a discussion about the way to implement a prod-uct feature. You disagree with it, think there is a better way to do it, and cannot believe how bad the suggestion was. Your natural reaction is to jump into the discussion, explain to everyone how this suggestion is wrong, and tell them about your suggestion and how much better it is.

The danger in doing so is that you would be acting on impulse. You haven't considered the perspective from the other side, and you think your idea is the best one. In such situations, be reticent and project calm. Your words and reactions will have an impact on your continuing ability to manage effectively.

Owning the gap between reaction and response means that you can train yourself to acknowledge an intense reaction to input—after all, these are human emotions. You may choose, however, to evaluate and decide an appropriate response for the situation. You can use mental trigger phrases such as "react and response" to remind yourself that you have acknowledged your reaction before you pause, think, and articulate a suitable response.

People will be looking at, listening to, and evaluating you. They will remember how you made them feel. It is plausible that, with time, they will not remember what you told them. They will, however, remember how your responses made them feel. Above all, stay calm.

Blaming does not help find a solution to a crisis. For the purposes of this book, a crisis is anything that may change the reputation of a person, team, project, or company.

You will need to address the cause of a crisis, especially if it is a recurring one; do so after a solution has been put in place, not while it is in process. Be careful, since you do not want to broadcast the message that it is not okay to make mistakes. It is okay to make mistakes; it is not okay to be careless or irresponsible.

Your projection of calm and confidence will empower the people involved to act. They will understand the gravity of the situation and will work with you to find a solution. By deliberately acting to own the gap between reaction and response, you open the door to becoming an inspiring role model to the people you work with.

Core Values

Core values are the foundation of a great team. They are like the crystallinity of the water in the reservoir and act as the self-control system for the minds of all members of the team. A code of conduct is important to define guidelines, but it is also an imposition, just as laws are. If someone wants to cheat the "laws," they will look for ways to circumvent them and won't feel bad about doing that—unless they are caught. Values, however, are part of the identity of the team and their members. Breaking a core value makes a person, and perhaps the team, acutely aware of the transgression.

A code of conduct is a punitive system. On the other end of the spectrum, perks are a reward system that is prone to cheating if the conscience doesn't react against the consequences of gaming the rules. Punishments and rewards may lead to perverse incentives and unintended consequences. There are countless examples where a rule is meant well, but its effects perhaps cause more harm than good.

It is imperative that the list of core values be short and that leaders and team members embody them. Failing to do so means that the values are meaningless, and no one will act in accordance with them. Some companies and teams list six, eight, ten, or even more core values. That is not realistic; no one will remember nor live by them all. The values are being set up for failure. They become an inconsequential space filler on a corporate communication or a team slide.

Optimally, there should be no more than three or four core values, and everyone, whether a new or existing employee, should agree to them. Declining to agree with core values would lead to an unsustainable relationship. It would be analogous to one person wanting to head north and another one wanting to go south. It would be impossible to satisfy both at the same time. When it comes to core values, every single person must be on board and in agreement with them.

These are my three core values:

1. **Integrity**: Stories are consistent and honest.
2. **Curiosity**: The employee needs to know the details about what the company and the team do.
3. **Determination**: Team members put in real effort and overcome obstacles to realize their accomplishments.

Paraphrasing Warren Buffet, if the person does not have the first of these core values, don't even bother with the other two. Integrity is the bedrock of trust.

When creating your own core values, go with plain and timeless language. Avoid jargon, buzzwords, or other terminology that will alienate team members or will not survive the test of time. Use simple terms that everyone understands. Corporate parlance is tribalist since only those who are familiar with the lingo will understand—allegedly. Its unintended (perhaps intended) consequence is to exclude those who are not in the inner circle. Everyone else will be left nodding their heads, pretending they understand what the values are and what they mean.

Along with the core values, you may choose to assign extra noncore values to your team or company. Note that those are complementary, just as food supplements add to rather than substitute for good nutrition. The way I see it, the difference between core and noncore values is that core values must not be breached, even at the cost of delaying a project or losing a customer. The supplemental values are more flexible and may occasionally be breached if and only if a context arises that can justify that. Although the noncore values have some flexibility, those exceptions must be infrequent, otherwise the value becomes meaningless.

For example, imagine that one of your company's additional values is craftsmanship and that there is a deadline you and your team cannot postpone. Trading the implementation of the feature for technical debt[1] would allow the product to be released on time. If this does not become the operational norm and is a rare event, one can make a justifiable case for breaching the craftsmanship value and accruing the technical debt. But don't forget to add an entry in the tasks backlog to refactor the code at the team's earliest convenience.

On another note, many companies have an unchanging rule that stipulates "No a**holes allowed." Granted, this is more a code of conduct than a core value, but I can understand why some may consider it a core one. We will talk more about this in the section on "Assembling the Team" in chapter 4. For now, I will just say that the cost of coping with such an individual is not worth your time and effort. The best option for you would be to help the person transition to a role or place where they would be a better fit and happier.

---

1   The most common form of technical debt is when parts of a system (code, frameworks, libraries, parts) are highly coupled to one another.

Make sure to define what being an a**hole means. Leaving it undefined keeps the door open to various and ambiguous interpretations. Without an explicit definition, a trivial everyday event such as you inquiring about the deliverables of a project, may be misinterpreted, turning you into what some might call "a tyrant." This is how I define an a**hole: someone who consistently and repeatedly shows one or more of the following traits—backstabbing, aggressiveness, intentional cruelty, tendency to seek advantages at the expense of others (zero-sum games), political social climbing, manipulation, or chronic complaining to you, to the team, or to customers.

Core values should be honest, not perfect. We are all humans, have flaws, and make mistakes. Be comfortable with our imperfections and know that it is all right to lapse occasionally. It is important to be aware that there is a gap between where you are and where you want to be. The core values should have room to accommodate that. Honesty will invite people to adopt and believe in these values.

Perks

Perks are tokens of appreciation for the team. Having perks as an employee and being able to offer perks as a company are great things. All those extras add up and make the place and the experience better. Beware, however, that the positive aspects of perks are not enough to hold the team together, nor will they retain top talent.

Employees will notice and will miss perks if the company does not offer them, but perks are not a reason in and of themselves to attract and retain talent. Many early startups and young companies cannot afford to provide perks, yet they are able to appeal to brilliant and high-performing employees.

Core values, as we have discussed, are the glue that keeps everything and everyone together. They imbue the team with intangible higher values and help align and unite everybody with shared beliefs.

It is great when the team has snacks, sparkling drinks, gym memberships, and so forth at their convenience. Some companies take perks to another level and offer housecleaning, laundry service, and more.

As appealing as they are, perks do not foster trust among teammates, do not create accountability for deliverables, do not motivate a sustainable productivity velocity, and do not inspire creativity to solve challenging problems. For that, a strong foundation with core values and meaningful team culture are the glue that binds a team. Top performers in your team are likewise not in it for the perks; they want to work on relevant material, projects, and tasks, and grow in their careers.

Patty McCord, the former Netflix chief talent officer who helped build the lauded culture deck, puts it this way in her book *Powerful: Building a Culture of Freedom and Responsibility*: "What people most want from work: to be able to come in and work with the right team of people—colleagues they trust and admire—and to focus like crazy on doing a great job together."

Top performers want to work on material and relevant projects and tasks and grow in their careers. Perks are just the glazing on top of the cherry, on top of the icing, on top of the cake. They are not essential but a nice luxury.

Culture

The bystander effect was popularized in the 1970s by Bibb Latané and John Darley in their work *The Unresponsive Bystander: Why Doesn't He Help?* Their study describes a tragic death where dozens of bystanders were in a position to act but failed to do so due to, among other factors, a "diffusion of responsibility" and the lack of a shared understanding of how to react in an emergency. The bystanders were law-abiding citizens, good people for all we know, yet none called the police to ask for help.

From this event, we learn that people's reaction to various situations does not evolve naturally. Instead, it takes deliberate choice to get a proper reaction. Much in the same way, great culture must be consciously defined and cultivated. It is not an organic process but a deliberate one learned through education.

You may be part of a small company, a large one, or somewhere in between. In all cases, your expectations should be that circumstances will not remain the same. Instead, you should assume that change is always happening and that without an established team culture, evolutions in scaling, longevity, and cohesion will be impossible or, at best, incredibly difficult. A culture will exist whether you created one or not. By acting upon it, you get the culture you want.

To begin with, culture must be designed; you do not ask what it should be. Culture is a strategic lever. The CEO of your company did it, and you must do the same. Adopt it, stay true to the existing culture, and expand it by defining the culture of your team. Failing to do so means that you would be losing one of your most important leverages.

But what exactly is culture? Let's begin with what it is not. Company culture is not about establishing rituals, getting the team together to have a drink, what you say, or the stories that you tell. One does not create culture with Ping-Pong tables or a snack bar. The answer to the question is much deeper and entire books can be written about what culture means.

In this book, I am narrowing the scope of culture to the perspective of management. I define culture when viewed as an aspect of management this way: culture is a common understanding and agreement among members of a team about how to address everyday challenges, tasks, and reactions to issues, ownership, accountability, and so forth. It is a source of guidance that is in alignment with the purpose of the company and encompasses decision-making that reflects core values. A large part of culture is how decisions are made when the manager is not present.

If you find your team members repeatedly asking how to perform a certain task, address an issue, design a feature, or something else, that demonstrates a culture is absent. Without a culture, actions and decisions made to address a range of tasks will take place without cohesion or coherence.

Members of your team should understand such situations and feel empowered to address them without feeling the need to consult you, yet they should have the confidence that they are prepared. This is in addition to regular communication, which absolutely must happen. In short, you should avoid being in a position where you are a choke point. In a good culture, team members know what the right thing is. In a great culture team members do the right thing.

When growing your team, hire people who fit the culture you implemented; if someone is not a good fit, that is okay. No one must adopt a culture that is not aligned with their behavior. However, they will need to find a different team or company to work for. Should they choose to leave, help the person find another place where they would be a better fit.

Talk to your team and establish common ways of evaluating designs, making trade-offs, implementing a feature, reacting to problems, and other things that are relevant to your operations. For example, completing a task starts before the task begins and continues beyond its implementation. A task may be defined as a larger unit composed of (1) architectural design, (2) documentation, (3) implementation, (4) quality assurance, (5) release, and (6) monitoring. With proper context and details, most of the uncertainties around the definition of a task dissipate, and the team can work together to do the right thing.

Culture also embodies the decisions you make when a proposition goes against core values. For example, should the team take a shortcut to meet a deadline and, with that, deliver an inferior product they will later need to come back to and refactor? I cannot answer this question for you. Irrespective of the answer, everyone on the team will be paying attention, and a precedent will be set that will either reinforce or erode the culture.

Setting goals and rallying to achieve them is another necessary culture-building practice. Sharing a common objective unites team members with the purpose of achieving them. That said, goals must not be imposed on the team but discussed and debated until alignment is found. People will only agree to dedicate time and effort to a goal if they participate in the process, are encouraged to contribute their opinions, and are heard and considered.

Establishing a culture and speaking of it once is insufficient. Habits need to be formed, remembered, practiced, and reevaluated. Continue talking to your team, refresh their memories occasionally, and mention culture every time you see an opportunity, for instance, during an event where context applies.

Managing Your Time

There will be many assorted activities, and there will be people demanding your attention. If you try to split your time and capacity to attend to all of them, it is likely that you will fail at most of them to some degree or another. In the same way, there is the natural tendency of the brain to work first on the easiest tasks, the ones that demand the least effort from you. Those activities trick your mind into believing that you are being productive, making you feel as if progress is being made because you are getting things done, right? At best, that is an illusion. You are prioritizing the urgent and the easy at the expense of what is important.

Begin by being specific about what you want to accomplish when you plan your time. If you are attending a meeting, what do you want to achieve at the end of it? If it is a task, how much progress do you want to make?

Whenever possible, cluster meeting schedules close to each other. Prefer the start of the day or the tail end of the afternoon. This will allow you to be in a single frame of mind and minimize switching context between meetings, other activities, and back to meetings.

Allocate blocks of time on your calendar to similar tasks that are applicable to your job. Meetings are one of the many activities for which you should plan and schedule time. For example, schedule an afternoon of meetings on architectural design revision and code reviews, then fit in a block of time for writing and replying to messages, a block for planning and decision-making, and so on.

That said, it is best to remain flexible. The reality of your days may confound the most determined schedule planning. There will be a variety of demands on your time, many of which you may have little to no control over, such as a system outage, a request from your manager, deliberations about the hue of blue for a button, and more. Among those unplanned demands on your time, you should be constantly evaluating where you can participate or not, and prioritize the ones where you can have the most impact.

There will be moments when you may feel uncomfortable about saying "no" to certain invitations to meetings, but that is a necessary part of doing what is important. You have a commitment to your team, your project, and your company. Saying yes to a request for your time and attention inevitably means saying no to something else. Practice the art of saying "no" in a polite and respectful way; there are many books and resources on this topic.

Be ruthless about controlling the time on your calendar; if you don't, something or someone will fill it for you. Letting your schedule get away from you leads to lower productivity during the day, and you end up having to make up for it by working nights, weekends, and holidays. In this scenario, you get burned out, and the quality of your work suffers.

I have adopted the practice of blocking time on my calendar for uninterrupted work. The length varies from sixty to ninety minutes depending on the task. The time slot will show as busy to others, and it is less likely anyone will request a meeting during that period. As much as possible, be specific about the activity and what you intend to accomplish when the time is up. With specificity comes productivity, accountability, and accomplishment. Without it, you may try to work on everything or anything and end up getting very little done.

Figure 2.1 approximates a typical schedule for my week. The number and names of people and some events have changed, but otherwise it conveys a deliberateness about organizing the activities on a calendar. Note that schedules with different purposes have different shades. This is not necessary, but in my case, it helps. By just glancing at it, I can tell the category of the activity. Each day also has enough unscheduled time for impromptu meetings and other tasks that will inevitably pop up.

Workweek

	Mon	Tue	Wed	Thu	Fri
9:00 am	Daily standup	Daily standup	Daily standup	Daily standup	Daily standup
9:30 am		Sprint Review	Company Training	Sprint Planning	Demos
10:00 am	Status report				
10:30 am	Team Planning		1:1 Peyton		Architectural Design Review, Roadmap Planning, Evaluate Decisions
11:00 am		EM:PM Sync		1:1 Finley	
11:30 am	1:1 Abayomi	OKR Review	Staff Meeting	Code Review	
12:00 noon	1:1 Manager				All Hands
12:30 pm					
1:00 pm	No Meetings Work Uninterrupted	Research Presentation	No Meetings Work Uninterrupted		
1:30 pm					
2:00 pm		Demos		No Meetings Work Uninterrupted	No Meetings Work Uninterrupted
2:30 pm					
3:00 pm	Infrastructure Updates			Product Release	1:1 Jannat
3:30 pm	Code Review	Code Review	Code Review		
4:00 pm					Write Weekly Summary
4:30 pm	Stakeholder Update	1:1 Taylor		1:1 Blake	
5:00 pm					

Figure 2.1: Calendar and Scheduling.

Effectively managing your time will not only save you the frustration of feeling unable to do what you intended to do but it will also allow you to work on what is important, such as managing the other streams. Time is your most valuable asset, and you must be disciplined in scheduling it. Failing to do so means losing control of your priorities and being pulled in many directions to work on other people's requests. Yes, you are a team player, and you should help when you are able to help. That is true only when you evaluate the request and conclude that you can have a meaningful impact. If not, perhaps someone else would be more effective for this request.

Remember, you have a commitment and associated expectations. At the end of the day, you need to have something to show for your participation or you have helped complete a task where you had the most impact.

Delegation

Sooner or later, you will be involved in too many activities and will have too many tasks assigned to you—more than you can possibly complete within the required deadlines. This poses a challenge: How are you going to be able to address it all? Working around the clock is not a viable option, and even if it were, you would eventually be stymied by the mere twenty-four hours in a day. Then what?

The answer is delegation, but it is far from easy. Here are a few of the reasons why:

- There will be tasks that you enjoy doing yourself and want to continue doing.
- You lose direct control of the task. It will not be done the way you would have done it, but you'd better begin accepting that as a fact.
- It may take longer to explain the task than to do it yourself.
- The person to whom you assigned the task may not be 100 percent ready.

Although valid justifications, none of those outweigh the fact that you need to be effective doing your job. The team, stakeholders, the company, and customers all have expectations related to your deliverables.

Begin by identifying what needs to be delegated and express it in the form of one or more tasks. Know, however, that there are tasks that cannot and should not be delegated. For instance, hiring and assembling the team and performance reviews should remain in your hands. On the other end of the spectrum are tasks that can be delegated. These include activities such as researching, evaluating, and proposing a new technology; preparing and presenting a demo; or being the scrum leader.

After the tasks have been identified, select the person who will be responsible for doing the job. Next, create the circumstances that will allow that person to be successful doing it. Then, provide as much specificity as possible. Provide examples of previous implementations of the task, if available. For example, if you are delegating the gathering of requirements for a new feature, share examples of previous documents showing the result.

Walk the person through the process you went through, and how you would do it if the task had been assigned to you—but leave room for the person to implement it differently. Be clear about what criteria for acceptance you consider when judging whether the task is complete. Reflect on what items are must-haves and include them. Transmit a clear sense of responsibility when explaining the purpose of the task.

Last, give the person autonomy to execute and agree on a cadence for checkpoints. Allow them to learn and grow doing the task, even if they are implementing it differently or suboptimally. If the difference is existential, give feedback, instruct them, and ask for specific points to change.

Delegation is not abdication of your duties; it is simply sharing the workload to make sure the work gets done. You will need to follow up periodically on the progress and give constructive feedback. After all, you are still accountable for the final deliverable. Keep in mind, however, that you are not the person implementing the task. Be respectful and understanding of the choices made by the person implementing it. Remember, you care about the outcome, not how you would have done it differently. If the result satisfies the acceptance criteria, accept it, and mark the task completed. Abstain from micromanaging.

Acknowledge and recognize the person's contribution once the task is complete. In addition, provide constructive and instructive feedback (we will explore "Feedback" in chapter 4). That will help the person grow professionally by understanding where their strengths and weaknesses were while implementing the task and will help you delegate more clearly and effectively.

Perfecting the reservoir lays the bedrock for effective leadership. By working on self-awareness, establishing core values, and prioritizing time, you shape a culture of purpose and clarity. These practices earn credibility and give understanding to those around you. Combined, these form a symbolic contract that legitimizes your leadership. As we move to the other chapters, we will explore how this disciplined self-management flows into the other streams.

CHAPTER 3

Managing the Reservoir: Decision-Making

You don't have to attend every argument you're invited to.

—Charlie Munger

The ability to make good decisions has a direct impact on the team, the project, and the company. What is more, decision-making plays an essential role in everyone's capacity for autonomy and for being able to take on more responsibilities. Explain to the team your rationale for proposing decisions, especially the ones that are repeatable by nature. By understanding where you are coming from and the mental model you used, team members will gain autonomy and learn how to decide when faced with similar situations. In the process, you will avoid becoming a choke point. The team will no longer need to come to you for decisions when they understand the principles on which it was based; they will need to keep you informed though.

Suppose a frequent decision you must make is whether to include tests in, say, a software product's code. Rather than having the team come to you every time a new feature is developed, you can gather everyone around (plus keep a record of it in the knowledge base) and explain your perspective on testing the code. For example, you could say, "By implementing tests in the code where we can simulate points of failure, it is possible to observe the behavior of the system before releasing it to customers. This allows us to implement safeguards to let the system fall back gracefully, rather than experiencing a crash or an outage, both of which would make for a bad user experience."

Ask whether everyone understands the basic principles of the reasoning and whether anyone has questions. Once the team understands the mental model for the decision and why it was made that way, they will later be able to decide for themselves what the right thing is. And since this will be recorded in the knowledge base, it can be used for future reference by both existing team members and newcomers to the team. Henceforth, the team will have more autonomy, and you will have more bandwidth to work on other more critical decisions.

Explain Your Decisions

Irrespective of a mental model or framework for decision-making, there must be an explanation to accompany a decision. You need to be able to clearly articulate the reasons for decisions. Before making any nontrivial decision, do one thing first: stop and ask yourself what the purpose of this decision is. You should have a hard-to-vary explanation to support your position.

The reason for having an explanation becomes clear when you share and talk about the decision with others, be they upstream, downstream, or lateral colleagues. You can only honestly and effectively persuade them when your description of the reason why makes sense and is hard to vary. By this, I mean you would do well to use explanations that cannot be easily changed or challenged.

A bad explanation in software development would be, for example, to say that a product is defective because the wrong programming language was used and language XYZ should have been used. Such an explanation is weak and essentially just stalls for time and adds confusion. In no way does it explain why the product is malfunctioning. For the sake of argument, even if the product were reimplemented using language XYZ, the problems would persist. The explanation can then be modified to say, "That was the wrong version of XYZ," or "Now, the best programming language is ABC, not XYZ." In contrast, a good explanation would be that the problems can be traced to the lack of thorough tests prior to releasing, and customers are the ones who are debugging the product.

British physicist David Deutsch has explored the concept of good explanations extensively. In *The Beginning of Infinity*, he writes, "Whenever it is easy to vary an explanation without changing its predictions, one could just as easily vary it to make different predictions if they were needed."

By stating that the product is defective, a subliminal message conveys that we are powerless to act and that there is nothing that can be done. This is self-defeating. Providing an explanation, however, shows that there is understanding and that addressing the question at hand is within reach. There is an invitation for action.

All knowledge contains errors, albeit unknown ones; nevertheless, they are errors. At the same time, knowledge with unknown errors is useful knowledge, and by no means do such errors imply that this knowledge is useless. History gives us countless examples of such situations. Until recently, Sir Isaac Newton's theory of gravity was our best explanation on the subject and was useful for solving many problems. Then Albert Einstein gave us the theory of relativity, which not only addressed the shortcomings of Newton's theory but expanded our understanding of gravity. There are likely shortcomings in Einstein's theory, but it is still our best explanation of gravity.

Treat your hypothesis and theories as the best explanations available to you at the moment. Use them in your decision-making process; if or when better explanations emerge, accept them, and adapt forward. It is impossible to turn back time, and it is not acceptable to sit idle and wait. It is often the case that the new, better explanation emerged precisely because you started with a worse one.

The mind of each person interprets how facts are understood differently. Only via good explanations can one minimize distortions, as it is impossible to eliminate them.

Our ability to provide good explanations is directly proportional to how much the subject in question is understood. Explanations can be questioned, improved, and mutated, and they can evolve when there is a better understanding.

In the 1960s, the technique used for computer face recognition consisted of measuring key metrics of a person's face, such as the distance from eye to eye and forehead to chin. There were several shortcomings to this approach, including poor recognition when the image was rotated or the head was tilted. Now we have much better techniques, and we can explain them much better, too. There is general acceptance that the current explanation is superior to the old one. This is not to say that the recent explanation is the final word or is as good as it will ever get. Far from it. The current use of technology is based on the best explanations that we have available at the moment—nothing more, nothing less.

In the future, there will be ever better explanations, with ever more accurate techniques. This evolution of the technology and technique would have not been possible if the viewpoints were based on observed facts. Those are immutable; they do not accept change. To put this into perspective, have you tried convincing someone that their favorite sports team is not as good as yours?

The reasons surrounding dogmatic decisions are easily varied and are adjustable to conform to the fact they are trying to support; advancements and progress become much more difficult under such circumstances. For every fact, there must be a corresponding explanation to support it. Dogmas crystallize information at a fixed point and become impervious to argumentation.

Allow me to deceive you for a moment and tell a lie with facts. What is the result of 2 + 2? Most people would say 4, and they would be right in most cases. But before you interject saying that 2 + 2 is always equal to 4, let me show you the facts in Figure 3.1.

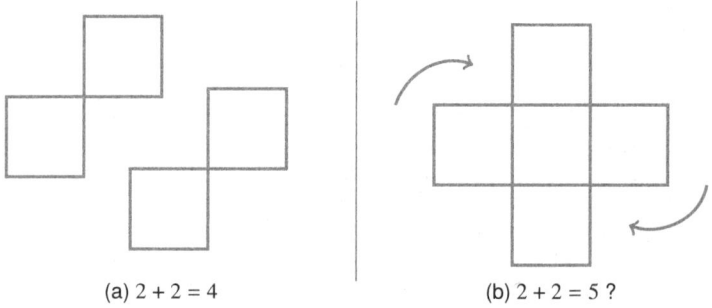

(a) 2 + 2 = 4   (b) 2 + 2 = 5 ?

Figure 3.1: Telling a Lie with Facts.

In Figure 3.1 (a) we see two squares at the top left and two more at the bottom right. When we add them up the result is indeed 4. Shifting to Figure 3.1 (b), the sets of squares are moved a little to the right and up, and a little to the left and down, as indicated by the arrows. "Undeniably" there are five squares. Is mathematics broken? Of course not. Although this may make for an entertaining geek joke, I misled you into observing facts and led you to a misconception. Only by having a good and hard-to-vary explanation can we prevent ourselves from being deceived. For starters, thinking that the lines defining the boundaries have any thickness at all is incorrect. Lines are infinitely thin; the drawing is just an artifice to help with visualization. Next, this only works with empty squares. Should they be colored on the inside, you would still see and count only four squares.

Another facet of facts is that they can be taken out of context to communicate something that is not entirely true or is misleading when the other factors are exposed. A few examples will make this clear:

- **Fact:** The local grocery store announces that the parking lot capacity has been increased by 20 percent.
- **Context:** The news turns negative when you learn that the feat was accomplished by reducing the spacing of each spot, rather than expanding into the lot vacated next door.
- **Fact:** Those shoes you were planning to buy are on sale at a 50 percent discount.
- **Context:** Disappointment kicks in when you discover that the discount is closer to 5 percent because the original price was marked up.
- **Fact:** A salary increase of 10 percent was the highest in years.
- **Context:** Inflation, on the other hand, was also 10 percent and erased all the gain in purchasing power.

A fact can only be accepted when its content is the same as our best explanations.

A trait of bad explanations is that their proponents often try to inoculate them against criticism. For instance, they may claim that those who contradict them are not worthy of being considered.

Always prefer good and hard-to-vary explanations. Even if those explanations contain unknown misconceptions, they still represent your best understanding of present circumstances. As knowledge improves, new discoveries are made, better explanations can emerge and, as a result, they will supplant the old ones. The misconceptions will only become known in hindsight, under the light of new knowledge and explanations. On the other hand, facts—and convictions based on facts—are static; they become immutable and ossified and transform into dogmas that cannot be challenged.

It may be tempting to disguise an explanation in vague statements that are nearly impossible to be proven false and that someone claims are a hard-to-vary explanation. One may have little to no knowledge about a subject and hide behind phrases such as, "This is a complex issue." Or they may say, "There are many factors to be considered," and so on.

A questioning technique used in a range of applications, from law enforcement to job interviews is the progressive inquiry that drills down and asks for ever more details in a story. Imagine a dialogue between a parent and their young adult child:

Parent: "Why did you arrive late?"
Child: "Because I went to watch a movie with my friends."
Parent: "What movie did you watch?"
Child: "The new *Sharknado*."
Parent: "What session did you go to?"
Child: "The movie started at 8:30 p.m."
Parent: "Who was the main actor?"
Child: "Oh, it was that guy from that movie. I missed the name because I went to buy popcorn and a drink."
Parent: "Do you have the receipt for the popcorn? What drink did you order?"
Child: "I tossed it in the garbage. I had a soda."
Parent: "What soda flavor?"

You can see that this conversation can keep going for a long time with the parent asking progressively more detailed questions. If the child had, indeed, done what they claimed, they would be able to provide the details.

If not, the explanations will become vague, and the story will fall apart. The same principle is applicable to explanations.

This may sound obvious, nevertheless it is worth saying: When you learn something, you acquire knowledge you did not have. Mastery of that subject goes hand in hand with hard-to-vary explanations. In essence, the more verifiable details you have, the harder it is to prove something false.

Speed of Decision-Making

The speed at which decisions are made is another determining factor of good and effective decision-making. I am not talking about reckless speed, nor impulsive decisions, rather, the tendency to decide quickly with a minimum of conviction and the ability to explain the decision.

First let's categorize decisions as: "easily reversible" and "not easily reversible." Most decisions are easily reversible; deciding reasonably quickly gives you the chance to validate the option you chose. If your choice was the wrong decision, you can pivot and try the other option or even abandon the initiative. Whichever the outcome, you will have learned something.

Conversely, taking too little time to decide incurs an opportunity cost; you will learn nothing, the gains from moving quickly could evaporate, and people on the team may become alienated. Being able to decide quickly, when applicable, can make the difference between a successful and unsuccessful endeavor.

Deciding slowly or not at all, according to Meg Whitman, former CEO of eBay and Hewlett-Packard, can cost a business dearly: "The price of inaction is far greater than the cost of a mistake."

Decisions that are not easily reversible are frequently accompanied by potentially severe consequences. If that is the case, of course, taking the time necessary to run a thorough analysis and talking to others is not only recommended but necessary.

Another aspect regarding the speed of decisions is the well intentioned, yet incorrect assumption that it is better to try to fit a new feature into an existing implementation of a product, rather than doing the necessary refactoring work to properly integrate it into the product. Anchoring the architecture design on the existing implementation with the premise of saving costs will lead to an inferior implementation that will frustrate customers. That will, in turn, give the competition an opening to present an alternative solution that is superior to yours. I call this the cost-avoidance bias. Yes, it absolutely makes sense to save on costs. However, parts of a system do not exist by themselves in a vacuum; the whole system must be taken into consideration in the analysis. Trying to save costs by developing a subpar product may ultimately prove to be very expensive.

The choices made to build a product in a certain way may have been the correct ones. Nevertheless, trying to fit a round peg in a square role under the erroneous pretext of building on top of what already exists may not be the best option. Refactoring parts of a system may be the right thing to do for the longevity of the product. It may be impossible and too costly to recover from the consequences of releasing something flawed to customers.

One of the products I worked on received a proposal from the team to implement a new machine learning model, in addition to two others that already existed. The functionality was new, and the model made complete sense. However, the design suggested that the risk scores of the new model be mixed with the risk scores of the other two models, even though the context of the risk scores was completely different. On top of that, the model was supposed to infer a minimum risk score of 80 percent—making false positives suddenly look a lot like an item of high importance. The suggestion was anchored on the existing implementation of the product, where the range of the other risk scores were mostly within the range of 80 percent to 100 percent. That would have made the user interface (UI) implementation much easier, by just slotting in a new result. But this came at the expense of the product's credibility. Fortunately, the feature was never released this way and that part of the UI was refactored to correctly accommodate the inference from the new model.

It is tempting to be in a perpetual state where you are open to any and all opportunities under the sun. You are always in pursuit of maximizing your options, continuously starting several new initiatives simultaneously. Inevitably, that leads to lack of focus with your effort being spread thin across projects; in this way, several initiatives are in the works, and none are complete. The business value of that is nonexistent. Even if each project has a relatively small value when complete, that still is infinitely larger in comparison to an unfinished one. The aggregate value of all those unfinished projects is zero, nada, naught. Until a product is finished, shipped, and used by customers, it is a cost center, rather than a revenue center.

This is not to say that you should remain closed to future opportunities in the decision-making process. First, for you, a new opportunity represents the future. Does it require immediate engagement, or can it wait its turn? Is it worth sacrificing your current responsibilities? Second, you feel a responsibility to complete your current project. Until the explanations for completing current projects are better than your temptations to diverge into building something new, put your efforts into delivering your existing projects.

Weighted Decision Trees

When faced with nontrivial decisions, assume that those are rational and that you have more than a few moments to analyze them. What is a good approach for making the right choice? This question may be impossible to answer; no one has complete information to be deterministic about the future. The best we can do is to adopt a methodology that will improve our chances of having made the right judgment. Weighted decision trees (WDT) are a framework I adopt in many situations where a clear option is not apparent.

You probably work with someone who often tries to find a flaw or an exception by saying, "What if the decision takes [insert unlikely scenario] and requires [insert unlikely requirement]?" As with any other situation, circumstances must be placed into context. If this framework is not a good fit for the decision it is helping to make, then an alternative one must be chosen. The crucial point here is that those teammates often, and repeatedly, raise unproductive and distracting arguments. We will talk more about managing such people in the section on "Managing Different Personality Types" in chapter 4.

Notice the differences in thickness on the edges connecting the decision nodes in Figure 3.2. The thickness indicates the likelihood of success based on your best knowledge at the time. By expressing your conviction as the weight of the lines, you mitigate potential bias toward a favored solution.

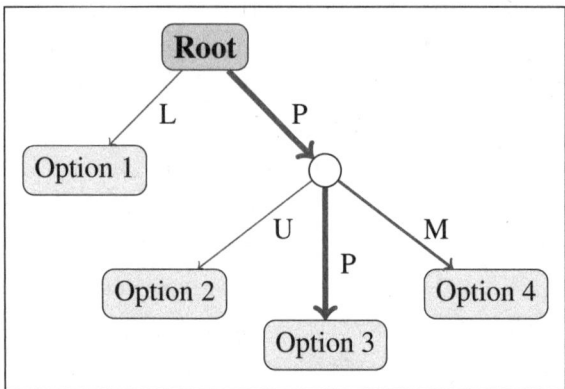

Figure 3.2: Weighted Decision Tree.

By now, you must be correctly assuming that to determine the weight associated with each edge, you will need to estimate the probability of success of each option. Well, that is impossible. Even imagining that we can predict such future probability is an exercise in self-deception. There are too many variables, and we don't even know what all those variables are.

The best we can do is use our experience to forecast based on the data and opinions available to us. Surprisingly, in most cases, that is enough for the purpose of decision-making. Remember that we are trying to make good decisions and not analyze ad infinitum until the best possible decision can be made. One might say that the cost of analysis paralysis is higher than the cost of a suboptimal choice. At a minimum, a decision will break the inertia and give you momentum, rather than leaving you stagnant. Even if wrong, it will allow you to learn from the mistake.

Opportunities expire. For decisions to be effective, they must be made within a reasonable time frame.

Getting back to weighted decision trees, a hazard of estimating the probability of an event's success is that it gives us a false degree of certainty. We may start believing that circumstances are under control. Rather than attributing numeric values to our estimates, I recommend using concept words that map to probability ranges. An example may make this easier to understand:

Success Category	Confidence Range
Unlikely	5%–15%
Low	16%–40%
Medium	41%–70%
Plausible	71%–95%

Table 3.1: Confidence Ranges for Success Concept Words.

Note that the probabilities do not go all the way to 100 percent. This is to reflect the fact that there are other unknown variables and that we have no way of estimating them. Depending on the uncertainty about the decision, you may choose to vary the ranges. Avoid, however, raising the ceiling deceptively close to 100 percent.

The estimates of success only need to be reasonably good. The longer you invest in deciding, the more it is going to cost you. Ask yourself how much accuracy is necessary for the decision at hand.

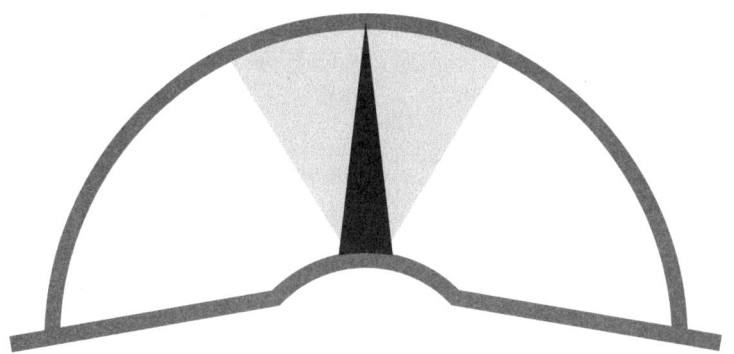

Figure 3.3: Decision Range.

Aim your decision to fall within an interval of correctness, as seen in Figure 3.3. With too little or too much investment in the decision, the quality will not be good enough or the cost will be too high.

Back to our decision tree in Figure 3.2, when drawing an edge from one node to another, attribute to it what you believe to be the likelihood of success. The higher the likelihood, the thicker the line becomes. It could be the case that the option you initially favored is less likely to happen when compared to other options, or perhaps your instincts were right all along. However, now you will have a stronger conviction with less bias. This does not guarantee the outcome or allow you to control exogenous circumstances or events. This framework is a tool to let you explore the possibilities and choose the option that theoretically has a better chance of a successful outcome. Here, success is defined as an outcome that closely matches your expectations.

To make a practical example, imagine that you want to choose the strategy for tests on the codebase. The root node represents our question, "How should we approach testing the codebase?" We can assume the options to be the following:

Option 1: No tests. We run the service on our computers and if it works here, it should work in production. This option has a low chance of success. Although luck may smile upon you once, what will happen when you make changes in the code? It may even work without crashing, but can you be certain that it is producing correct and consistent results?

Option 2: The QA team is responsible for running all the tests. This option has an unlikely chance of success. It is not scalable for every release, and it would only test the parts of the code activated via a user-interface interaction.

Option 3: Implement tests and integrate them with the continuous integration (CI) system. This option has a probable chance of success. There will be automated tests that run periodically, every time new code is merged to the codebase. If a change introduces a bug, there is a good chance that it will be captured by the tests, causing them to fail. You will be able to fix it before shipping the product.

Option 4: Implement tests and run them on a developer's computer. This option has a moderate chance of success. Although better than no tests, a developer may forget to run the tests, versions of the libraries may be different between the developer's machine and the build system, and there is the possibility of encountering the dreadful bug of "but it works on my computer."

Looking at the options and their descriptions, it may look as if Option 3 is the obvious choice for our example. In reality, however, the situation may be more complicated. What is the cost of implementing a continuous integration system if one is not already in place? Although such a system is highly recommended, an upfront investment would need to be made. If the context is a small startup with few resources to build the proof of concept (PoC) of their product, perhaps the right choice in this case would be Option 4.

With more complex decisions it is only natural to expect more complex WDTs with several nodes and edges, leading to cases where you may ask yourself what the chances are of Option A and Option B to happen (i.e., the chance of both outcomes taking place). In another case, Option A or Option B (i.e., one of the outcomes happens, but not both).

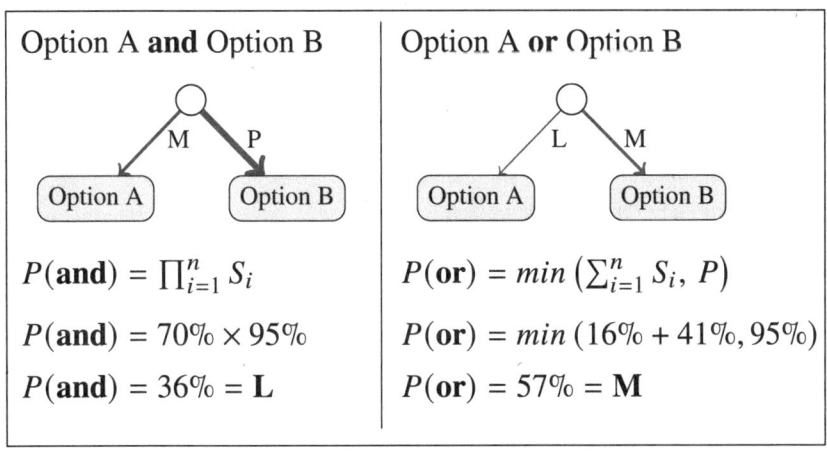

Figure 3.4: A and/or B Options.

On the left-hand side of the illustration above, we see that the probability of both Option A and Option B happening is the product of their chances of success S_i. The chance of success of Option A is medium (70 percent) and for Option B the chances are plausible (95 percent). Their product is 36 percent, which places the expectation of both Option A and Option B happening in the low range.

On the right-hand side, we see the case where the probability of Option A or Option B happening is the minimum between the sum of their chances of success and of being plausible. Note that odds cannot be higher than our maximum confidence, nor should it be possible to total more than 100 percent. The chances of success for Option A is low (16 percent), and for Option B, the chances are medium (41 percent).

Their sum is 57 percent and the minimum between 57 percent and 95 percent is 57 percent. This places the expectation of either option happening in the medium range.

Note that for the product operations [and] I chose the upper value from each chance-of-success range, and that for the sum operations [or] I picked the lower value of each range. This is an optimistic approach regarding the odds and my preference. Perhaps you will choose the midpoint from each range. Whichever values you pick, be consistent. Avoid having one preference for certain decisions and a different preference for others; in this case, you would be introducing bias.

Consider factors in the context of the outcome from the decision. In a purely rational and probabilistic decision-making process, no one would ever launch a product or start a company since the odds of success are low. The decision-making process approached here has little to do with chance. People do start companies and launch products, and that has to do with product-market fit, the skills and the ability of the teams to work together, and other factors.

The W's of Decision-Making

Begin by asking yourself some questions before deciding. They will clarify the topic at hand and facilitate understanding about which goal the decision aims to achieve.

- What decision needs to be made? This is the most important of the questions. Recognize what you are trying to address and the impact of the decision. Make a decision that leads to an action that implements what you wanted done.
- When does it have to be made? Is it important, urgent, both, or neither? Focus your attention on the decisions that are both important and urgent.
- Who will decide? Are you the decision-maker? Or are you part of the decision-making chain and need to provide information for an informed decision? If you are not the decision-maker, what information would you like to have to make this decision? Share the information with the owner of the decision.

- Who will need to be consulted prior to making the decision? Gather the information you need to make the decision. Reach out to the team, peers, and whomever else may have key data or experience to advise you.
- Who will need to be informed of the decision? Communication is paramount. Inform the team, upper management, stakeholders, and other parties who would benefit from the knowledge of it.

Listen attentively to criticism made during the conversations prior to the decision being made—and after it's made. Only by accepting criticism and discovering imperfections can you improve upon an idea. Criticism, when meant well and done honestly and respectfully, is a sign that someone cares. The best way to criticize is to discuss the central points, refuting or accepting them. Ad hominem labeling and name-calling are not valid forms of criticism; in practice, they should be discouraged and disapproved.

In general, people only criticize topics they care about and want to improve. There may be too much information and too many ideas circulating in the many spheres of your universes—team, organization, company, city, state, country, and so forth. Plus, time and attention span are too scarce to care enough to analyze and criticize them all. Therefore, it is only logical to assume that when someone gives you feedback on an idea or conversation, that is because they chose to spend their time on something they care about and want to improve upon.

When you listen, resist the urge to respond. Stay silent, pay attention, and digest everything that is being said to you. In the end, say thank you and express your appreciation for the input. Acknowledge that you understand the intention and want to make things better. This way, people will feel comfortable and empowered to keep giving you feedback in the future.

This is not to say that decisions should be made by committee—not at all. By listening, you are considering perspectives and narratives that you may not have considered and perhaps are complementary to the decision at hand. Those opinions and criticisms may positively influence your decision.

We will examine more about committees and consensus in "Is This a Democracy?" in chapter 4.

Better than Chance

The outcome we all expect from decision-making is that we will do better than chance. To put this into perspective, imagine that the alternative is playing the wheel of fortune and each of your options is placed on equal-sized slices of the wheel. You give the wheel a spin and hope for the best. That would be a terrible way to proceed.

All the techniques and frameworks we examined in this section compel you to consider the inputs from others, account for different possibilities, investigate the data, exercise discernment (using your accumulated professional experience), and develop hard-to-vary explanations.

Even though there are no guarantees that a decision will be the right one, we can still consider that your decision is the best one at this moment, considering the context. And that is why, even if it was incorrect, you would learn from it; the experience will contain knowledge and that will help you do better next time. When decisions are made without careful consideration or are left to chance, they do not carry knowledge since there was no hypothesis, degree of conviction, or explanation.

CHAPTER 4

Managing Downstream: Team

The most difficult thing is the decision to act; the rest is merely tenacity.

—Amelia Earhart

The most important task of managers is to make sure their team delivers results. Great managers do that in a sustainable, ethical, and transparent way. Here, we will look at how to do that, starting with building a team, establishing core values, communicating transparently with them, fostering growth, addressing members who are not performing to expectations or may not be a good fit, and more.

Downstream management includes not only managing the team members who report directly and indirectly to you but also managing projects and operations. There is much to say about this category, thus Downstream has been organized into three chapters: Managing Downstream: Team, Managing Downstream: Project, and Managing Downstream: Operations.

A significant part of your time will be allocated to managing the team, and that is a good thing. Your team comprises the people who implement the product and make things happen. They are the creators, operators, and executors. In your time with them, communicate clearly and patiently, both when listening and speaking, to give and receive feedback, gather and share information, and create the circumstances that will enable them to be successful.

Assembling the Team

Conventional wisdom says that you should hire great people and leave them alone. Although there is truth in that, such advice is incomplete. When assembling your team, you want to be strategic in choosing the talent according to what everyone brings to the table. Throughout history, there are countless examples of stellar teams that could never work together and in the end were unable to deliver. Why?

The reality is that those teams were not assembled to work together. They lacked synergy, and the sum of the parts was smaller than the whole. A well-designed team needs members who fulfill various roles, have different internal motivations, and bring a fair amount of overlap to the skills needed for the mission.

When looking to attract and retain talent, look beyond the technical skills and qualifications each person contributes. A great team has members who are driven by disparate motives. Look for and assemble your team with, at a minimum, the following roles:

- **Visionary:** The term is being used here in the sense of inventors. These are thinkers who come up with ideas and solutions to problems and challenges, including but not limited to product features, customer requests, and improvements to existing systems. They play a vital role in influencing and giving shape to the product road map. This person can be you, an engineer, or someone else on the team with both technical knowledge and broader expertise in the area.
- **Problem-solver:** They know how to transform a concept into a product or service. Problem-solvers can implement, scale, and troubleshoot a system. A better mousetrap is always in the cards for them.
- **Forwarder:** People who remain focused on tasks until they are complete; they take visions and implementations across the finish

line. They are disciplined and continue the mission until the work is done, rather than losing interest and switching to another project after only 80 percent of the current one is complete. The problem here is that results only count when they are delivered.

To make this clear, let me ask you a question. What is more important in a car, the wheels or the motor? The answer is both. Without wheels a car cannot move, and without the motor a car does not have propulsion. We are assuming that a typical car has four wheels and one motor. An equivalent principle of ratios applies to the roles we are discussing. All roles are important, but the number of people needed for each of the roles will differ. A team needs a tiny number of visionaries, a larger number of problem-solvers, and a moderate number of forwarders.

There are more kinds of motivations and roles you could add to this list. For example, a connector—someone who knows how to bring together key people to talk the talk and walk the walk. You will either need to have larger teams or members who possess two or more of those motivations. Those people are not only rare but also demand premium compensation, many times worth every penny.

There is one kind of team member you should avoid at all costs: the chronic complainer. (Add to the list the intellectual-only and the intellectual-only chronic complainer.) General George S. Patton may have been thinking of complainers stuck in stasis when he famously said: "Lead, follow, or get out of the way." Chronic complainers do not want to lead, follow, or get out of the way. Instead, they want to tell you about all the obstacles, the problems with everything, and how none of what is being discussed or has been done is going to work. The same goes for the intellectual-only. Chronic complainers disregard the possibility that the people on the other side of the conversation may already be aware of the issue and have been working hard to address it. Complainers propose no viable solution, nor do they take any initiative to fix the problem.

Pointing out problems and not knowing how to solve them yet is perfectly acceptable, if people do so with the genuine intent of rolling up their sleeves to get the necessary work done. The team may need help to do so, and you as a manager have the responsibility to help coordinate that. What is important is a positive attitude and the conviction that leads to taking ownership of the task to eventually find a solution.

The Interview

As you prepare to screen candidates, meet with your HR counterpart to explain what you are looking for in terms of technical expertise, behavior, and role on the team. As you interview candidates, do your best to identify their motivations and how well they fulfill the requirements. Once their motivations are identified, ask questions that invite candidates to tell stories to describe and highlight them. Formulate questions that best reflect what you are looking for in a candidate. Here are a few examples to get you started:

- **Visionary**: "Tell me about the vision you have for that product."
- **Problem-solver**: "What was the biggest challenge you've experienced while implementing a key feature you enjoyed working on?"
- **Forwarder**: "Tell me the story of releasing that feature."
- **Connector**: "Explain how you moderate conversations among team members?"

When someone speaks about their motivations and has been working on them for long enough, there will be a lot to say. They will certainly have stories to tell. Listen attentively to the answers because you will learn a great deal about the candidate.

Keep asking questions to learn more about skills, teamwork, craftsmanship, and more. Look for discrepancies or holes in the narrative. If you run out of questions because the candidate had solid answers, you may have found a 10x candidate. Be prepared to make a competitive offer because candidates like these do not come by every day.

Even if you do not run out of questions, the candidate still qualifies to continue the discussion. What are the skills you are looking for? What personality type would fit best with the team? What personal values align with the team and company values? Depending on what you have heard during the interview, the candidate may be just the person you are looking for.

Consider reassessing your initial opinion of a candidate's motivations throughout the interview; it may be necessary to adjust course and switch questions to a different topic.

As for the complainer, ask, "What would you fix in your last project?" If the candidate is an opinionated armchair expert, and you feel the floodgates of negativity open, thank the candidate for their time at the end of the interview and send a follow-up message saying that you have decided not to move forward.

The following are general themes to both guide your company sales pitch to the candidate and formulate your interview questions to evaluate whether the candidate is a good fit:

- Explain the reason why we [the company] are building these products and how the candidates see themselves fitting in.
- Describe the short-term road map (three to six months) for some of what is to come. The candidate is transparent about what they will be doing, and you get a sense of excitement from them.
- Describe the role, priorities, and your expectations. Be direct to candidates and ask if they can see themselves doing the job.

As much as we all want to believe it, there are no universal polymaths; if there are, they are extremely rare and would not be the kind of person interviewing for jobs. It seems, however, that they are in abundance, given the requirements listed in this fictional job posting:

The ideal candidate must have proficient knowledge in rocket science, computer programming, corporate law, accounting, fly-fishing, industrial design, plumbing, car racing, boat racing, molecular biology, ice hockey, quantum physics, horse riding, project management, guitar playing, helicopter skiing, biofuels, robotics, literature of Medieval Europe, recycling of rare earth minerals, electronics, and the bovine digestive system.

In the unlikely event such a person exists (Please send me a message if you are real; I would like to meet you!), we are all constrained to the same twenty-four hours in a day. There would be no time to learn all those skills, acquire all that knowledge, and engage in all those activities. Focus on the core skills you are looking for and a candidate who excels in those.

Meet the Team

Welcome to your team! The following people are your fictional direct reports for the purposes of this book. You will see them show up in examples going forward. Take some time to get acquainted with the people who work for you. Pay attention to their specialties, personalities, passions, hobbies, and any other interesting facts about their life.

Abayomi	Back-end engineer who joined the company about two years ago. Abayomi has a degree in computer science and since an early age has been fascinated with computers. Traveling is a personal passion, as are string instruments. Abayomi has visited several countries to learn the many different sounds made with strings.
Blake	Machine learning engineer passionate about the technologies that enable humans and computers to work together, leveraging the best each can offer. Blake has a PhD in machine learning, always has a new article to share, and often speaks at conferences. During his free time, you may find Blake riding an off-road bike or tinkering with the drivetrain for fast and smooth gear shifting.
Finley	Self-taught back-end engineer with a determination to do what needs to be done to complete a project. You will see Finley the happiest when a project is shipped and in the hands of customers using it. Books are a constant companion, from thrillers to books on technical subjects—in audio, print, or electronic format. Some say that Finley's personal library is like a backup to the local public library.

Peyton	Front-end engineer who has been writing code since computers used floppy disks. Peyton has a degree in mathematics and joined us after completing a yearlong stay in Antarctica experiencing life among penguins on the least populous continent on the planet. Peyton's passion is to build products at the intersection of form and function.
Jannat	Mobile engineer who is a polymath in the many languages and technologies used to develop the major mobile OS platforms. Jannat studied physics in college and is a great proponent of explaining how to implement features, from mobile components to back-end and API design. During his free time, Jannat is a family person and, on the weekend, a softball coach.
Taylor	System architect and software engineer with the mind of a visionary and the work results to support it. Taylor studied philosophy in college and has a knack for proposing solutions that address the challenge at hand and have an elegant architectural design. Animals, especially dogs, are among Taylor's passions outside the office.

Table 4.1a: About the Team.

Your team does not have to be comprised of extraordinary people. It must have people who accomplish extraordinary things. Those people are the ones who build the products customers will use to make their lives better.

Maslow's Hierarchy of Needs

In 1943, American psychologist Abraham Maslow published a paper called "A Theory of Human Motivation," in which he proposed the idea that humans have universal needs. Those needs are both material and emotional. He represented the hierarchy of needs as a pyramid, where basic needs build the foundation; the higher you go, the more abstract those needs become, until they culminate in self-actualization.

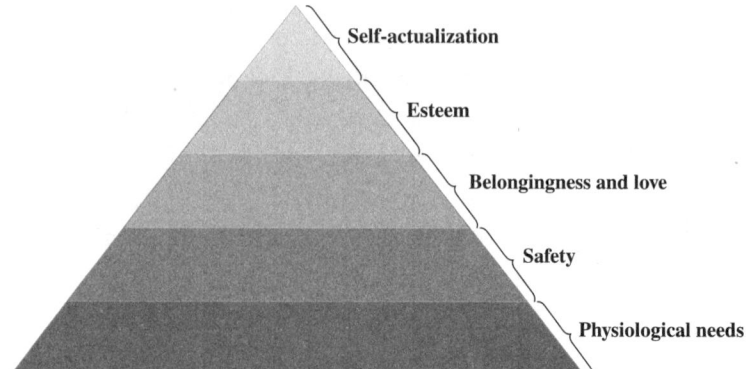

Figure 4.1b: Maslow's Hierarchy of Needs.

The hierarchy of needs is composed of basic needs at the foundation, psychological needs in the middle, and self-fulfillment needs at the top of the pyramid. Starting from the bottom and working our way to the top, here are some examples of each of the needs:

1. **Physiological needs**: Food, water, warmth, and rest.
2. **Safety**: Security, shelter, resources.
3. **Belongingness and love**: Being close to family and friends, joining a society or group, being part of a team.
4. **Esteem**: Self-confidence and respect from peers. Wanting to be recognized for contributions. Motivation to perform and to compete is at the highest.
5. **Self-actualization**: Living according to one's potential, guided by the persistent impulse to be all you can be. Pursuing goals.

It is important to notice that one cannot skip levels. To reach safety, one must first satisfy physiological and other needs.

The path to self-actualization is a personal journey. I don't believe a manager can do much to help a team member get there, except taking care to avoid being an obstacle.

As a manager and a leader, work to create the circumstances where your team can prosper and grow: Make sure everyone has an adequate working environment. Make them feel safe and help them belong to the group. Once they are part of the team, they are ready to stand out and excel.

It is common practice in many companies to have a small pantry with some items. A few companies have complete kitchens that serve an entire meal. Whatever your company can afford, it is a good idea to have good and healthy food available to your team.

An adequate working environment includes proper equipment, adequate environmental conditions, and emotional support. The equipment you provide to the team—computers, monitors, chairs, desks, and the like—should be of good quality. How would you expect high-quality output if low-quality equipment says otherwise? The working space should be clean, organized, illuminated, and temperature controlled. Last, but not least, every person has the right to be respected and treated well when they go to work. No one deserves to be mistreated; appropriate behavior is a must.

There are many ways to help members of your team feel that they belong to a group. Hackathons, milestone celebrations, branded apparel, themed dress-up days, shared meals, book clubs, and study groups are a few of them. All these activities foster solidarity and reinforce trust among team members. These activities address much more than team morale. They help build rapport, create strong relationships, and facilitate communication.

Another benefit is that they help mitigate politics. As we know, politicking is debilitating for teams. It erodes trust, transparency, communication, and ultimately results. When strong relationships are created among members of the extended team, you may avoid hearing negative generalized phrases such as, "Engineers only care about code," "Sales doesn't care about product quality," or "Person X never collaborates."

Ownership

"Ownership" may sound like a contradictory term in teamwork. After all, a team collaborates in a shared effort aimed at achieving a goal. How can someone "own" something allocated to the team and the company? This is one of those situations where context must be applied to avoid misinterpretation. In the context of a team, ownership signifies feeling a sense of strong responsibility for the outcome, not possession.

A clear delineation of the ownership of features, tasks, and responsibilities must be established for all team members. This means that each task has a particular person accountable for its completion and delivery, rather than someone being the sole proprietor of a part of the product to the extent that no one else can get near it. It will often be the case that one person will have ownership of a product feature and, concurrently, a group of people will be actively working on it.

Assignment of ownership begins with a conversation with the team in which everyone discusses what needs to be done. Team members will either naturally gravitate toward owning a task or will be assigned to one as planning progresses. Collaboration becomes easier when directions are well defined and accountability is crystal clear.

A couple of topics need to be discussed prior to the assignment of ownership: the definition of "done" (certain criteria are used to accept a task as complete. See "Release Process" in chapter 6) and how to disagree (establish the rules of engagement for discussions when ideas collide). To help interactions become smooth and professional, rules could cover issues including trust to speak and listen, transparency, respect for each other, permission to make mistakes, and no blaming.

> **You**: Following up on our conversation, data extraction is the next task for us to work on. Do we have any suggestions on how we're going to implement it?
>
> **Taylor**: Yes, we will implement an API to interact with other parts of the system. We need to specify an end point, parameters, data structure and so on. The service also needs to apply data transformation to format it to be compatible with the rest of the pipeline.
>
> Who can take this task?
>
> **Abayomi**: I will take it. I haven't implemented a new API since joining, so this is a good opportunity for me to build one from scratch.
>
> Here's my plan: I will write a page with how this will work, implement the changes, include validation tests, add a chart to the dashboard, and release once everything is working.

Sample 4.1: Assigning Ownership.

In Sample 4.1, there is clarity and understanding of what needs to be done and clear ownership of the task. After this conversation, you can create tickets to formally assign responsibility and follow progress. The formalization of an assignment is typically done via a project management tool, where a ticket is created having a detailed description of the task; this should include acceptance criteria for completion and assignment to the person who owns it. We will explore this in more detail later in the section about "Planning" in chapter 5.

Two other ingredients that need to be present are autonomy and resourcefulness. Team members need to be given autonomy to design, implement, test, and solve problems without having to ask for permission. Autonomy does not mean to act as a rogue agent, independent from everything and everyone. It is necessary that this is coupled with the expectation of frequent communication, which then allows all parties to evaluate alignment with goals and intent. There should be no secret projects or concealed actions. Lack of communication would reduce transparency, erode trust, and eventually lead to the curtailing of autonomy.

Of course, there will be many times when team members will come to you to discuss ideas, talk about decisions, ask for help, etc. This does not contradict autonomy; it is part of the process. Ultimately, you are part of the team. This would only be an issue if the team did not have autonomy and had to come to you as the manager every time, all the time, for everything. You would unwillingly become a non-scalable choke point to the project.

The team must also be resourceful. This includes, but is not limited to, researching techniques to implement solutions, contacting other teams and stakeholders, speaking up when help is needed, and so forth. Idly waiting for "something" is not acceptable, no matter how good the excuse. Find, ask for, or help with another task.

When you empower your team to act autonomously, to be resourceful, and keep an open channel for constant communication, you are treating them as responsible adults. The sense of ownership becomes natural and not contradictory at all.

If ownership needs to be transferred to someone else, communicate explicitly that the transfer is happening to all parties affected. Some cases may be as simple as reassigning a ticket from one person to the other after a quick chat. Some other cases may need a knowledge transfer session where specific information pertinent to the task can be passed on and questions can be asked and answered.

Is This a Democracy?

What is a democracy? The philosopher Karl Popper proposes that democracy is a system that allows for the removal of policies and rulers most efficiently, without the use of violence. The democratic aspect of a corporation is that employees, including managers and executives, may be removed or replaced if they underperform in their jobs.

We all want to be friendly and on good terms with all team members. We also would like to be perceived as good managers. Yet, there will be moments when team alignment on a certain topic is unattainable and a decision must be made. You are the decision-maker.

Note that I mentioned alignment and not consensus. In the context of this book, "alignment" occurs when the intent is clearly understood and the expected output is shared among members. "Consensus" happens when a majority agrees on a common approach to execute a task or decide which tasks to execute; consensus is about compromise, not about doing what is right or what needs to be done.

An example will illustrate this distinction: Imagine that a group of people are asked to reach the top of a mountain. The intent is clear: reach the summit. We say that there is alignment among them. The next step is figuring out how to get there. If all participants decide to hike to the mountaintop, we say there is consensus. However, that is not a necessary condition for completing the task. If, instead of hiking, some decide to ride an off-road vehicle, others board a plane and skydive, and still others prefer some third option, there is no consensus about how to reach the summit. But there is still alignment that everyone should meet at the top.

When faced with a situation in which a decision will upset or frustrate one or more people on the team, an instinctive reaction may be to avoid conflict and shift the narrative to, "We're a democracy here." This is an abdication of leadership. Although this may make the situation a little more comfortable for you right now, in the long run, there will be a high price to pay.

A corporation is not a democracy, nor should it be. Neither is it a tyranny. This means decisions should not be made in the spirit of "my way or the highway." As a manager, you cannot know all the information and all the perspectives behind decisions, which means you should engage in conversations with the team, stakeholders, and others, depending on the nature of the decision and any confidentiality requirements associated with it. The people on the team are the ones implementing the product and bring perspectives that consider even the smallest details. Stakeholders will consider other aspects that may include other products, target market, budget, and so forth. Their input is meant to be useful in influencing your decision, not in making the decision for you.

Keep in mind that you should aim to get it right, not to be right. There will be inputs and perspectives from other parties, such as product managers, designers, subject matter experts, and customers. This will allow you to be aware of a broader range of angles and considerations, all of which will better equip you to make the best decision you can, given the information and context available at the moment.

Managing the expectations of those on your team is critical, especially the expectations that come with being part of the decision-making conversation. Being among those having the conversations means that members of the team will share their perspectives and their knowledge of the product with you. It is your job to hear their voices, concerns, obstacles to execution, and so forth. All those factors will shape the decision you have to make. It should be clear to the team that decisions are not made by consensus but by your informed decision.

The role of decision-maker should be clear, and although you will have that responsibility most of the time, depending on the circumstances, someone else may share that responsibility. The decision-maker is not a dictator and is not a committee spokesperson either. You are required to consider inputs, opinions, and suggestions—but you are not required to include them in the decision. This dynamic should be communicated to the team so that all members understand it.

Before any decision-making takes place, you may want to have a conversation with the team about what your expectations are after a decision is made. Inevitably, there will be team members who will disagree about what was decided, and although that is perfectly fine, you will need to speak to them and acknowledge that you heard, understood, and considered their input. Nevertheless, you need their full cooperation in the implementation of the decision; no sabotage of any sort is welcome or productive. If these members criticize the decision, do not give in because they will pull in the opposite direction of the team. The chances of success are reduced, and, in the end, the team and the customers are going to be the ones who suffer the most.

It is okay for some members to disagree. Disagreements are not only expected, they are key to a healthy discussion. A healthy discussion is dialectic—all participants want to get to the best decision via reasoned argumentation. Everyone should understand that, after a decision is made, continued disagreement becomes a divisive and corrosive force.

Assume for a moment that you choose to go against the advice given here and instead opt to run a democratic process by voting to find a consensus. The votes of the people with incomplete information will count, as will those of low performers and those who are proposing an incorrect approach. Consider an unpopular decision such as switching technologies or terminating a project. Those invested in them are most likely to favor maintaining the status quo. There will be plenty of excuses and justifications concerning why the group should not go through with the changes; after all, the opponents are defending their investment of time and effort. The perverse incentive is to maintain the status quo, without making changes. At the end of the process, you will find yourself in a position where you need to live through and deal with a situation that is suboptimal—perhaps even wrong. How are you going to explain that to stakeholders? How are you going to justify it to customers?

You may argue that in an ideal world, the right thing to do would be to support what is best for the project and not what favors someone's best interest. Where do you find those altruistic angels? How do you recruit them to the team?

Choosing not to make a sound decision when one is needed and instead going with the majority may lead to lack of accountability. You as the manager may say, "I was just following the team's suggestion," and the team may say, "We were just presenting our suggestion to our manager." Neither side accepts blame for a bad decision.

It is equally important to steer clear of compromising in decision-making when contemplating two competing ideas (A and B). One may initially think that finding a middle ground combining the best parts of A and B would produce a good outcome.

There are a few problems with that thinking. First, the combination of each idea is, in fact, a third option (C) that no one supports. Second, each proponent has an explanation for why they believe their idea would work. Third, if C fails, no one will have learned anything because there was no explanation to validate the idea. People will be none the wiser and will go back to supporting A or B. In fact, it is more likely than not that C would fail because neither of the proponents will be fully dedicated to it. After all, that is a third option with no explainability to support it and no one feeling enthusiastic about it or committed to it.

Instead of compromise, choose the idea with an explanation that seems to have the best chances of success, and then commit to it. Of course, it is possible that the option you picked will fail, but at least you will have learned something in the process because there was a hypothesis, an explanation supporting the idea. In such a case, acknowledge that the choice did not work, discuss the lessons learned with the team, and pivot to implement the other idea.

It is also possible that the product idea you picked will work. Once the product is built, and if there were great elements in the other idea, you can always ask the team to implement those elements to complement the product.

Do the right thing. It is your responsibility to own the decision and get your team on board to implement it. Explain your thought process, the path that led you to it. Although some may not see eye to eye with you, they will understand and respect your decision.

Meetings

Meetings are moments where a manager can listen to the team, communicate a message, and use the time either to gather information for decision-making or to ask for decision-making feedback.

Before each meeting, you should ask yourself who needs to be in the meeting and invite only the people who must attend. It is common to see meeting invites going to many people, even though not all those people will be able to add value to that meeting. If you weren't the organizer of the meeting and there are too many members of your team among the attendees, ask the organizer whether all those people must attend. If the answer is no, then ask the organizer to reduce the number of participants to the absolute minimum.

One needs approval for expenditures beyond a certain value. The same person, however, can organize a meeting and invite a large crowd, in essence, spending more than the approved expenses threshold. Meetings cost time and money, so make sure meetings are productive and pay for themselves.

Individual contributors need long, uninterrupted stretches of time to be productive. As much as possible, try scheduling meetings at opportune moments when disruption is kept to a minimum. For instance, try to schedule meetings in the morning, after lunch, or at the end of the day. This should, however, be the least preferable option since the IC's mind is already fatigued from a day of focusing on complex work. You must also account for differences in time zones, schedules, and more.

You should host and attend as few meetings as possible, but not fewer. That is, you should be selective and only attend those meetings that have a clear purpose and add value.

When you are organizing a meeting, prepare an agenda with the purpose of the meeting and the expected outcome. Also, forward all relevant material to attendees in advance so they may become familiar with the content, prepare their questions and/or contributions, and evaluate whether their presence is needed.

During the meeting, make sure that voices are heard. It is common to have one or more people who speak more fluently and end up occupying more of the airwaves. Make sure that you address people by name and solicit their input. They will appreciate that, and you will have gained another point of view.

If you are communicating a message, expressing your point of view, or stating a course of action, ask the people attending for their reaction. Under no circumstance should you let the meeting end without explicit feedback from the attendees.

And when it is time to end the meeting (keeping to the allotted time as much as possible), ask if anyone has anything to add, summarize the reason for the meeting, mention the agenda items covered, and ask attendees if they got what they wanted from the meeting. In the event you did not cover everything or the meeting did not satisfy expectations, ask yourself whether a follow-up meeting is needed. You may have enough from the meeting to move forward. Schedule another meeting only if you absolutely must. Avoid booking another meeting just for the sake of completing a discussion. As tempting as it may be, use your best judgement to avoid extension meetings.

Many discussions can take place via email or instant message, rather than during a meeting. Often, one just wants to express an idea, report an issue, or discuss some other matter where team feedback is necessary. Instead of booking a meeting and asking all attendees to contribute their time (remember the monetary and productivity costs), write a message summarizing the subject and soliciting feedback. This way, recipients can respond any time it is least disruptive for them to do so. As a manager, you must be clear to your team that radio silence is not an option and that a timely reply (twenty-four hours or less) is required. Be unambiguous about this and the trade-offs between a meeting versus a message and be clear that you expect all recipient team members will be active participants, even if to say that at that moment they have nothing to contribute to the discussion. This practice will save you and your team the loss of valuable time and productivity.

Special Meetings

There are two kinds of special meetings with your team: one-on-one discussions and staff meetings. For the one-on-one meetings you should ask your direct report to prepare an agenda in advance to talk about things on their mind, career growth, professional issues, developing a network, contributions, and more. You should also have an agenda, but only bring your items into the conversation after you both have covered your team member's items. There will be times when that person's agenda will take up the entire meeting; there will be other times when the reverse is true. Try to maintain a two-way conversation as much as possible.

Staff meetings are an opportunity for you to do the following:

- Discuss the road ahead.

- Define core values.
- Assess team performance.
- Evaluate the market and competition.
- Talk about alignment of vision, autonomy, and ownership.
- Address specific issues such as expenses, politicking, company policies, conflict resolution, and technological or other challenges ahead.
- Recognize accomplishments and celebrate milestones.
- Address actionable items.
- Share news about the team and company.
- Discuss work-life balance.
- Answer questions.

Sustainable Productivity Velocity

Between 2018 and 2019, I spent a considerable amount of time collecting data and studying the impact interruptions have on productivity. Interruptions can include unnecessary meetings, unexpected context switching (shifting from one task to another), and system failures as a result of technical debt (hacks and shortcuts over craftsmanship). All of those negatively affect the production capacity of a team, and although we all have our opinions and suspicions about how much or to what extent productivity is affected, these are just our opinions, our gut feelings, most likely not supported by data. Therefore, there is no foundation to prevent avoidable interruptions nor incentive to regain that lost productivity.

We can measure, quantify, and model the data to have a deeper understanding of the extent of the impact. Perhaps more important: Can we determine what can be done about it?

In this section, I present the key insights from this study. The results show the clear costs of avoidable interruptions and the impact they have on productivity and even quality of life (when people work at odd hours just to keep systems operational). Note that I am not advocating to remove all meetings, task switching, and technical debt; that would be unrealistic. The point I am making is that by knowing the real costs, you can choose the trade-off.

For technical details, including equations, more graphs, and how the results were calculated, please see Appendix A: Sustainable Productivity Velocity.

Interruptions can be of a planned (stand-up meeting) or unpredictable (service disruption) nature. For the rest of this section, I am going to use the word "incident" to represent any kind of interruption, regardless of its nature.

One of the properties of the data is that incidents are mostly independent from one another. By that I mean that an interruption caused by a system outage is independent from an interruption to attend a meeting to hear from a guest speaker. However, there may be correlated interruptions, such as a postmortem meeting following a system outage.

From the data I collected, modeled, and plotted in Figure 4.2, we can see that the probability of observing two incidents in day is almost 25 percent. This means that the expectation of being negatively interrupted is constantly on people's minds. It is not a matter of if, but when (how soon) the next incident will happen.

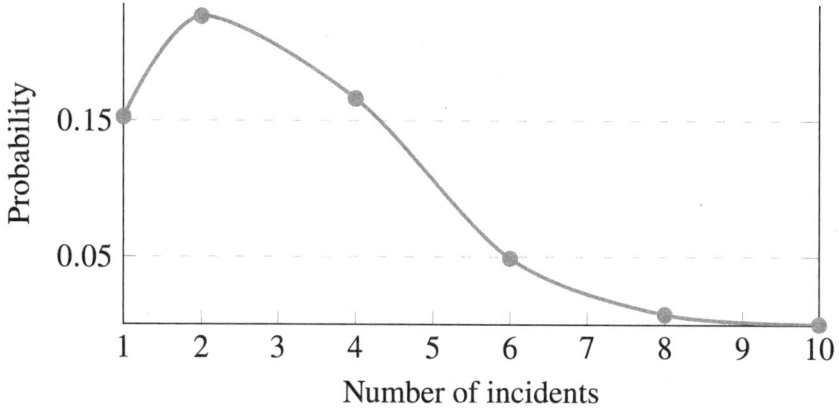

Figure 4.2: Probability of Observing k Incidents in One Day.

In addition to computing the probability of an incident occurring over a given time period, we can also compute the probability of waiting a certain amount of time until an incident occurs.

Figure 4.3 tells us that the chance of having an incident-free morning and making it to lunchtime without negative interruptions is smaller than 30 percent.

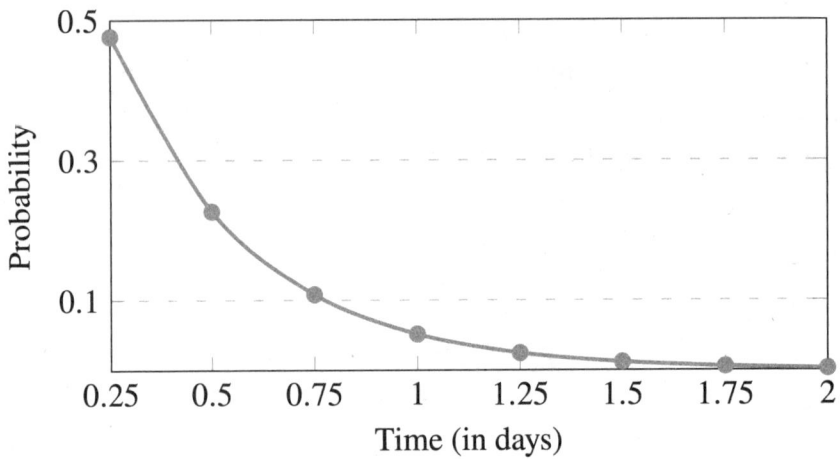

Figure 4.3: Probability of Waiting More than t Days for an Incident.

You can already see a theme emerging here. The more care is taken to avoid incidents, the more the team's productive capacity increases. Good architectural design, quality code, test coverage, timing of meetings to allow for large, uninterrupted blocks of productive time—all of those contribute to higher output and happier teams.

Here, we introduce the concept of productivity velocity V. In physics, velocity is defined and measured as a change in distance over time. In the context of productivity, velocity is the change in progress developing a product over time.

$$V(t) = V_0 e^{-ut}$$

In equation 4.1, V_0 is the initial productivity velocity. We can assume it to be 1, or 100 percent, at the start of a project since there are no incidents yet. In the event of an ongoing project, V_0 is the average of all points scheduled for a sprint.

The constant of proportionality u is the factor by which the velocity decays with the passage of time t, due to incidents negatively impacting the productivity capacity of the team.

Note that u is negative. This means that incidents have an exponential adverse impact on the productivity of a team.

Throughout the course of a project, there will be several sprints. If we look at a large enough window of time, meanwhile allowing for the impact of incidents to continue, it won't take long until the productivity of the team grinds to a halt.

The productivity of an engineer and of a team is directly proportional (strongly correlated) to the amount of uninterrupted time dedicated to working on the tasks.

Let's work on a practical example. Assuming that over the past six sprints, Blake has delivered an average of fifteen points per sprint. During the planning meeting, Blake committed to thirteen points for the upcoming sprint.

According to this estimate, it would take Blake about 86 percent of a day to complete two points, leaving 14 percent of the day for other activities. Those other activities would be best if scheduled at the beginning or end of the day (or at least before or after a lunch break) to allow for large blocks of uninterrupted time. Any other scheduling would have a large negative impact on productivity.

When someone is interrupted the loss of productivity is immediate. Regaining momentum, however, takes a while. This dynamic of loss and restoration of productivity can be seen represented in Figure 4.4. Assuming that productivity is at its peak in the time range between 0 and 2, we can imagine that if an incident occurs at point 2, it will cause complete loss of velocity. The time between points 3 and 4 is an estimate of how long it takes to address the incident.

When resuming work, productivity is not restored immediately, it takes some time for one to get back to the mental state prior to the incident and regain the same level of productivity. This recovery period is represented by the sigmoid function plotted in the interval between 4 and 14. (The sigmoid function has a characteristic S-shaped curve, here meaning the acceleration period to resume full productivity.)

Fewer incidents bring an increase in velocity, simply by freeing time that would otherwise be spent in an unproductive manner. Your team alone will not be able to take action to minimize those incidents. Often, they may feel bad (guilty) for not joining a meeting or not switching context to work on a random task when asked. You, the manager, are likely the only person in a position to act, therefore you must lead and

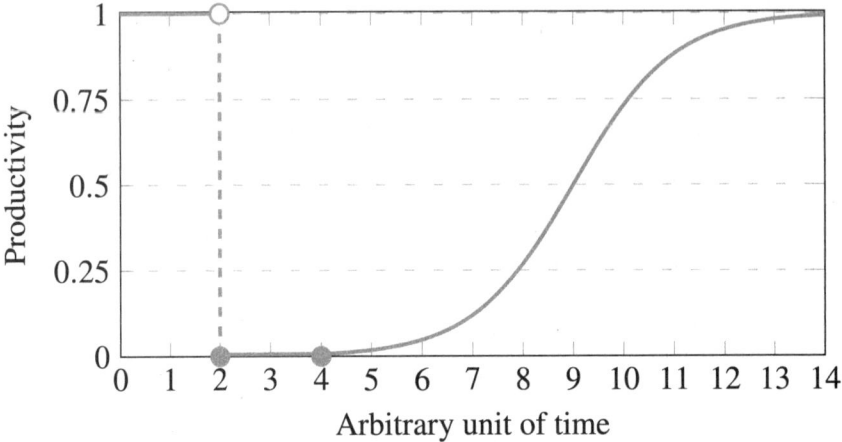

Figure 4.4: Resuming Productivity.

put a deliberate effort into creating the circumstances where the team can maintain a sustainably high productivity velocity. Establish a policy that it is okay to question the need to attend certain meetings, ask for some conversations to be scheduled in advance, and to direct whoever asked them to switch tasks to first speak with you.

The lesson here is to avoid, to the extent possible, unwanted, unsolicited, unexpected, and burdensome distractions that add severe friction to productivity. It is unrealistic, and even undesirable, to operate at 100 percent all the time; only by truly understanding the costs of incidents can you make conscious trade-offs, including deliberate moments of downtime to rest and to have fun.

Onboarding

A new team member, upon joining your team, does not know the key people to talk to, the details of what they are supposed to do, or what the manager's expectations are in general. It is your job to create an onboarding journey that is welcoming and sets them up for success.

Begin before they officially start. Contact them and make yourself available to answer or find an answer to questions. Then explain where they will fit in with the team and what impact their work will have on the product. Next, tell them about the technology and tools used in the products; give them a list of topics they may want to review prior to day one.

On the first day, post an announcement that your team is welcoming a new member. For larger companies, the scope of the announcement may be your department. In the case of smaller companies, you may announce it to everyone. A good message would include a paragraph in which you introduce the new team member and one or two paragraphs about where they share a little about themselves, their background, and a short fun story about them. Here is an example:

Make room on the red carpet and hold the paparazzi cameras. Today I am thrilled to welcome Jannat to our team. Jannat is an accomplished software engineer, having worked on the Flux Capacitor and the Tardis. Here are a few words from Jannat:

"Hello everyone! My name is Jannat and I have just joined the company. Most recently, I worked as a software engineer at Time Travel, where I started on the recommendations team and then moved to the analytics side. I am located near the Rocky Mountains, and skiing is a passion of mine during the winter. In the summer, I like to ride my bicycle and play the guitar. Super excited to be here and can't wait to meet all of you over the coming weeks and start contributing to building great products together."

Sample 4.2: Onboarding Message.

The next step is to share a list of people with whom the person should meet. Include engineers, product managers, marketing people, legal staff, and more—basically anyone who you think would add context and knowledge or would often work together with Jannat. In addition, set a deadline for the new team member to meet with everyone on the list. Starting a conversation is often a task that throws us out of our comfort zone, thus it is easy to consider this task low priority and, thus, keep postponing it. One way to make this and other tasks easier is to assign another team member to be the newcomer's welcoming buddy. Nevertheless, keep following up in your one-on-one conversations until the person has met with everyone on the list.

There will be other steps, such as how to connect to the network, where to find the codebase, how to obtain permission to access files. The list can be long, and some tasks will be specific to your company. Prepare written instructions with all the important steps, and, to the extent possible, organize them in the order they should be executed. The instructions should be published on the company's knowledge base system. Make sure it is accessible to everyone inside the company, and share the link with the new team member. As with most documentation, there may be items that become outdated and, thus, lose value over time and are never updated. Encourage the new team member to edit and update the document as necessary.

Sample 4.3 is a simple onboarding document (often called the "Getting Started" document). Your version may contain more steps, have links to other documents, and so forth:

Here, you will find a compilation of all you need to know to complete the onboarding process: reading materials, training, environments, and other information that will enable you to find your way around. You will find instructions for accessing the codebase, data, systems, and more. Check with your buddy and/or manager if your questions are not addressed here.

General Onboarding Tasks
- Verify that your credentials are valid and that you can log in to the system.
- Complete the new hire orientation.
- Complete the mandatory training.
- Verify your access to the internal company portal. There, you will find links to company essentials, such as HR, Q&A, benefits, and more.
- Make sure you know how to use the ticketing system and how to request services, equipment, and other work-related items.

IT Onboarding Tasks
- Request access to the knowledge base, ticketing system, and code repository.
- Ask to be added to the videoconferencing system.

- Verify that your email and messaging software are working.
- Familiarize yourself with how to schedule meetings and reserve conference rooms.
- Update your profile.

Sample 4.3: Sample "Getting Started."

Perks such as backpacks, shirts, and pens are great. If your company offers them, by all means, make sure that the new team member has all that is offered. Although welcome, those perks do not help the new employee with ramping up, learning what is expected of them, and where and how they are expected to contribute. Helping them navigate their first steps at the company and having clear expectations are immensely important. This is notably more valuable than any swag in their welcoming kit. Prepare a document with your expectations and meet with the new team member to go over them. It is much easier to succeed when one knows what is expected of them. Sample 4.4 is an onboarding expectations document for the first 30/60/90 days.

This document is a reference point to set expectations and for us to keep track of your progress toward those goals.

Expectations are a communication of intent, rather than immutable goals written in stone. A list of actionable items will guide us over the next weeks and months. The list will be the reference document to your new position and a road map to a journey where you are continuously and increasingly successful, together with the team.

Expectations

Joining a new team involves getting to know the people, learning about the product, becoming familiarized with the codebase, and more. These are milestones that will help guide you through the journey.

The First Two Weeks

The first few days are said to be the hardest. Almost everything is unknown. Let's invest time in the following:

- Meet all members of your direct team.
- Learn what the projects are about, their missions, and how they bring value serving our customers.
- Become familiar with the tech stack and standing it up in your development environment.
- Make a symbolic contribution to the codebase.

After Thirty Days

Around this time, you start finding your bearings. The people are now familiar, you have a better understanding of the project, and the tech stack is no longer an iceberg mostly hidden beneath the surface. At this point, you will be able to do the following:

- Make technical contributions to the project.
- Have your first pull request merged to the mainline, or have something shipped to production.
- Participate in technical and product conversations and articulate your point of view.
- Meet with more than 70 percent of the people on your list of colleagues to meet.

After Sixty Days

You are becoming a pro. At this point, you will be able to or have completed the following:

- Make suggestions about the technology, frameworks, and implementation.
- Be an active participant in code reviews. The most effective way of doing a code review is to understand the intent of the other person, then evaluate whether the code implementation matches it.
- Propose architectural designs and documentation.
- Implement quality control tests that not only verify the functionality but also try to "break" the system to assure that

there is a graceful fallback when the system is put to work in ways it was not intended.
- Have met with all on your list of people to meet and have grown your network beyond them.

After Ninety Days
The sky is the limit. You are an effective member of the team.
- You are fluent in the tech stack.
- You have completed a product release yourself.
- You have written diagrams and documentation.
- You have a network of colleagues across multiple teams.
- You know how to effectively produce and consume metrics (e.g., dashboards, logs).

Sample 4.4: Onboarding Expectations.

Last, but not least, present a general overview of values, team, projects, road map, and miscellaneous topics. This can be either a direct conversation with the new team member or a team-wide refresher (if it has been a while since you last spoke about it).

In your presentation, consider including slides for the following topics:
- Team values.
- Career growth.
- The simultaneous importance of both craftsmanship and shipping products.
- The understanding that everyone has a voice. Opinions are welcome and will be heard. Decisions will consider those opinions, but in case of disagreement, you still need everyone's commitment and to be onboard.
- Autonomy, communication, and transparency.
- Overview of existing products.
- Future features, products, and potential road map for them.
- Simplified organization chart with key stakeholders.

Gamification of Performance Metrics

Performance metrics may be a double-edged sword. On one hand, they provide measurements of important aspects of the health of the team and the project; on the other hand, they give the illusion that adherence to the metrics alone is enough, regardless of the broader context. Besides, there is the unintended consequence of trying to game the system.

Even with the downsides, my preference is to use metrics. They provide vital monitoring information. It would be unimaginable to fly a modern airplane without instruments. With just an instrument or two, there would not be enough data to do the job. Picture in your head a dashboard with only a speedometer and a compass. How would a pilot know the altitude or how much fuel is left?

Being aware of the downside of metrics is important because it helps you identify then mitigate potential negatives. The same is true about knowing the downside of anything. The downside itself does not invalidate the tool, method, or idea. That said, having knowledge of it will be useful in avoiding hazards and getting the best out of the process.

Gamification, in this context, is a strategy for the team to attain and maintain a sustainable level of productivity and quality. It uses elements of game principles to measure the output and health of the team.

It is paramount to focus on the sustainability of the strategy adopted. If your metrics are always trying to maximize output, the team will burn out and likely leave. At the other end of the spectrum, if the metrics are too relaxed, productivity and engagement will be low. Finding a sustainable balance is key. This also means that the metrics are far from remaining as is. They will need frequent adjustments and reevaluation.

For a team of engineers, I found that the following metrics have worked quite well to maintain a balance between productivity, quality, and life outside work. Let's examine them and discuss why they are appropriate choices.

Number of Commits: This measures the number of contributions made to the codebase. One may feel tempted to make several unnecessary commits to inflate this metric. We reach balance by combining it with other metrics measuring contributions. Too few commits may indicate disengagement.

Number of Reviews: This measures how many code reviews were completed. A code review verifies and provides feedback to the contributions made by other engineers. This is a metric of teamwork, accountability, and quality of the product. One may try to provide shallow reviews, but other members of the team will be quick to raise the lack of meaningful participation. In the same way, that may signal absence of commitment to the project.

Number of Merges: This measures the number of contributions that were reviewed and merged to the mainline of the product. Many merges may indicate that accountability and quality are on the backseat. Not enough merges indicates that the project may be stalled and features are not being delivered.

Number of Tasks Completed: Measurement of how many tasks from the current sprint and/or backlog were completed. This is planned work in collaboration with the product team. Ideally the number of tasks planned for a sprint and the number of tasks completed are close to each other.

Number of Research Projects Concluded: Contributions are more than code committed to the codebase. Engineers often need to research a topic, explore the data, or learn a new framework. This is a proxy metric for the professional growth of the team. It indirectly measures how much they are learning and keeping their skills up to date. Too many ongoing research projects may come at the expense of progress on existing projects. Too few and the team may not be learning enough or growing professionally.

Number of Actionable Items from Research: The research project should be concluded with a recommendation, positive or negative. There is nothing wrong with a negative recommendation; sometimes it is better to know that option A is not the best choice. This metric is an accountability metric to bring research to a conclusion, rather than let it run for an indefinite amount of time.

Number of Issues: This measures the number of issues encountered or reported in a product that has been released. Problems found before release are not counted here. Except for a small number of issues, this metric may indicate that you need to invest more in quality control.

Number of Days Off: People need to take time off and unplug. You don't want your people always functioning at peak performance. They will burn out and eventually leave the team. Time off is an important metric for the health of the team and work-life balance. Too few days off is not healthy and that person is in danger of burning out. Too many days off may signal lack of commitment or perhaps that someone is about to leave the team.

Number of Team Activities: As we learned in Maslow's hierarchy of needs, feeling that you belong is important. Team activities bring people together. Too few may lead to individuals working on a project, rather than a team with shared values and purpose.

I am not aware of any tool able to compile and display those metrics. They may exist; I am simply not aware of them. I use a spreadsheet to collect and keep track of the data, and you may consider using one, too. Table 4.2 shows a spreadsheet with all the metrics discussed here.

There is no ideal range for any of the numbers. You need to learn what is right for your team and work to maintain consistency of the observed metrics over time. Monitoring and acting on them will give you levers you did not have before. The aim is to have a highly productive team, a high-quality product, and great work-life balance. What is more, you will gain better insight into high and low performers.

Week in Project	Number of Commits	Number of Reviews	Number of Merges	Tasks Completed	Research Concluded	Actionable Items	Number of Issues	Number of Days Off	Team Activities
Week 1	51	8	4	10	0	0	0	1	0
Week 2	39	3	4	7	1	0	0	0	0
Week 3	65	11	6	11	0	0	1	3	1
Week 4	74	8	5	8	2	2	0	0	0
Week 5	52	6	5	10	0	0	0	2	0
...	...	...	...	...	...	...	...	...	...
Week n	70	7	6	6	0	0	0	0	1
Total	351	43	30	52	3	2	1	6	2

Table 4.2: Team Health and Performance Metrics.

High performers come with their own broad set of challenges: keeping them engaged, offering opportunities for professional growth, and recognizing their work with rewards and acknowledgments. Recognition and acknowledgment of their contributions should be items often present on your radar. These can include shout-outs, public praise, and promotions that should first go to them. Rhetoric of gratitude to the recipients, and an unambiguous message to the team regarding what success looks like.

Regarding the low performers, you, or someone else in the company, made the choice to invite them to the team. They showed technical, behavioral, or other qualities that were strong enough to earn them a place on the team. Before considering anything drastic, give them some very specific feedback (see the section on "Difficult Performance Feedback" later in this chapter) and set clear expectations about what you expect to see as output from their work and behavior. If, however, the situation does not improve over time, come up with a transition plan, and let the person go. See more about this in "Letting People Go," also in this chapter. Last, but not least, do not reward low performers. It is not the right thing to do, and it would not be fair to all others on the team.

These metrics alone are not sufficient to evaluate members of the team, but they constitute a major consideration. Other items, such as collaboration with other teams, impact of the contributions, and ability to communicate and negotiate ideas effectively also play crucial roles in evaluating each person.

Feedback

Feedback is one of the most important and powerful tools a manager has at their disposal. At the same time, it is one of the hardest to use effectively. There must be a relationship of trust between a manager and a direct report, a peer, or an upper manager, otherwise feedback may easily be confused with confrontational criticism.

It is most likely that you won't be able to perform the job better than your direct report. You will nevertheless be observing them and will be able to provide valuable information that will help make them even better at their jobs.

The purpose of feedback is to give someone information that becomes an actionable item for their improvement and growth. Feedback is not about saying whatever is in your head; that would just be releasing frustrations over past events and would add no value to the conversation. Feedback must be constructive and specific. It is meant to improve the future.

It is common to see feedback categorized in management literature as either positive or negative. But I prefer other terms that are more aligned with the true nature of feedback—constructive feedback and instructive feedback. "Constructive feedback" is given when the person is expanding on something that is already good and in progress. "Instructive feedback" is provided when there is lack of awareness in an area where the person has the potential to improve or stop doing something.

Feedback is more than highlighting weaknesses and working toward improving them; that is a small and less valuable part of the feedback process. The goal of feedback is to provide actionable information to your people in the areas where they can become even better by continuously developing their skills to new higher levels. By becoming aware of something, they can act upon it and develop themselves further. An important part of your job is to make sure your team is growing and becoming better. Feedback is one of the best tools for doing that.

Constructive feedback should be given in proportion to instructive feedback. When someone does something good, don't miss the opportunity to let them know what was done well.

When providing feedback, be as specific as possible, whether you are giving constructive or instructive feedback. For example, when providing constructive feedback, instead of saying, "Great request. Keep up the good work," be more specific. You could say, for example, "The way you wrote the description explaining how the code changes in the pull request affects the system behavior made it much easier for the team to review the refactoring."

When giving instructive feedback, rather than saying, "You rushed your presentation," provide details in your comment such as, "You were speaking too fast and moving the cursor too abruptly. Attendees could not follow your line of thought and were distracted by the hurried movement of the pointer."

Either way, the person will know the full context of the feedback and will be able to act on your information. Your team members want to be accountable. They want to know how to grow and improve every day. It is part of your job to let them know and not let them fail.

A pitfall to avoid is delivering several pieces of feedback at once. It may become overwhelming for your direct report to digest everything at once. Instead, pick the top two pieces of feedback, preferably constructive and instructive feedback, and communicate those to your direct report.

Be unequivocal when you are switching context between constructive and instructive feedback; you don't want the messages to be mixed. and you want your direct report to understand each message clearly and distinctly. Leave the remaining feedback for another occasion.

Be honest and transparent in your conversations. If something is right, say so. If something is not right, express that as well. Be specific and describe with details and examples. Your team will be grateful for your candid feedback. That will help them grow and become better professionals.

The most difficult feedback is when you need to have a hard conversation with an employee. Be mindful that both of you are people and, as people, you have emotions. The hard conversation must happen; things will not improve by avoiding or delaying the conversation. Be prepared by writing down your talking points in advance and rehearsing the conversation in your mind. Be honest and transparent. The person must understand where you are coming from, and you must understand that individual's perspective. State your expectations, so it is clear what corrective action is needed.

Difficult Performance Feedback

There is also the kind of feedback you must give to any low-performing team members. You have to believe that the feedback you are providing will have an effect and will enable them to bring their A game. If you think the feedback will not help, that the issue is more than working harder or putting in more effort, it is better to be transparent with the person and find an amicable manner to part ways. Keeping the person around is not fair to the other team members. The most talented people on your team will be among the first to leave when mediocrity is allowed to settle in and grow roots. After all, they have the confidence that another company will hire them if they leave the team, and a few may even start their own companies.

Some conversations need to be followed up with a written message, such as the one shown in Sample 4.5. The purpose of the message is to bring specificity to the conversation and a clearer understanding of what is being addressed. The teammate may not be able or know how to improve on their own. Come up with a plan with specific actions for that person, and you can follow progress during one-on-one meetings.

Managing Different Personality Types

There is only a small chance that you chose everyone on your team. The more common scenario is that you hired some and others were already part of the team. Or you might have been assigned to a new team whose members were there before you.

In all those circumstances, you will encounter a variety of personality types and will need to manage team members differently. Here, we are looking at personality types from the narrow perspective of a manager. In Figure 4.5, at one end of the spectrum of personality types, we encounter those who are high performers and whose efforts are aligned with you and the project. At the opposite end, we find those who are low performers and are applying their energy in diverging directions.

Aligned, high performer   Misaligned, low performer

Figure 4.5: Spectrum of Personality Types.

Let's look at the extremities, then at those in between, and see how they can be managed as a variation of the extremes.

Given that there may be countless personality types, it would not be feasible to analyze and create a custom approach to each one. Instead, by studying and addressing each end of the spectrum, we can come up with a couple of frameworks that may be sufficient to cover the whole gamut. We can make an analogy with a shoestring held at both ends by their tips. If we lift them at the same time, all that is in between will be raised as well. By addressing extreme cases, there is a good chance, not a guarantee, that the middle will have been addressed as well. However, there may be exceptions where you will need to address them on a case-by-case basis.

We begin with what is one of the biggest challenges: managing high performers. Their productivity is higher when compared with most team members, and their efforts are aligned with the objectives of the project. Such people thrive in their professional careers. They want to grow, reach the next level, and become even better. It is easier to understand when we draw a parallel with the career path of athletes. Some students will do so well at their school that they will go to the state championship and nationals, and they might even receive a college scholarship. Continuing their progress, a few might qualify for the Olympics, win a medal, hold an Olympic record, hold the world record, or break their own world record.

The journey of a high-performing team member is no different than that of a star athlete. And although not directly mentioned, we know that the athlete did not achieve it all alone; they had support from many different people from family to coaches and sponsors. For the talents on your team, it is your job to help them advance and reach higher. You may not be with them for their whole career, but you will have made a difference in a chapter of their lives.

Talk to them about their career and ask how they want to grow. Give them an assignment that involves learning a new skill or another they would not be able to complete alone and would need to seek help from others, such as for research and development of a proof-of-concept project. There are many more tools at your disposal to continually invest in their professional development.

> **You**: Finley, the work you've done to implement data streaming has had a massive impact in our ability to distribute the processing across multiple nodes. But I noticed there's something else you wanted to do. What is it?
>
> **Finley**: I'm glad you asked. Even though processing is now fault-tolerant and can be distributed among multiple nodes, what happens if there is an outage affecting the whole data center? I wanted to learn more about disaster recovery techniques and how to distribute the traffic across data centers.
>
> **You**: There is an upcoming conference in parallel and distributed computing. Why don't you look into the details, including ticket, airfare, and hotel, and give me a budget for attending the conference?

Sample 4.5: Managing a High Performer.

Now let's switch gears and look at the challenge of managing low performers. It is often the case that those team members have difficult personalities; they are often combative and defensive. However, it is highly unlikely that they are bad people. On the contrary, it is more likely that they are good people who battle so intensely for their personal agenda that it generates friction and misalignment with the project and the other team members.

Their attention and arguments gravitate toward the way the world should work, rather than the way the world works. Their idealism becomes exaggerated, and their preoccupation shifts to how they want things to be. That puts them at odds with how things are, and, as a result, their work suffers. Their unwillingness to accept much has a direct and corrosive impact on everyone. You may hear symptomatic excuses, such as, "But I have high standards." The problem with statements like these is that we all have high standards, however, many struggle to accept that and react badly when those standards are not met.

I am reminded of something that AngelList founder Naval Ravikant said: "Pointing out obvious exceptions implies that either the target isn't smart, or that you aren't."

Another symptom may be chronically pointing out imperfections or shortfalls in the system. More likely than not, the people on the other side of the criticism are already aware of the issues and have been working on implementing fixes. The critics, on the other hand, almost always fail to propose a solution that works better, is more economical, and can be implemented.

Although they are not bad people, the actions of low performers can be a destructive force in the team that negatively affects everyone's morale. Avoid trying to please them publicly. Direct your focus to high performers because dealing with a low performer is rarely productive.

At the same time, address those team members in private conversations. Listen to them, ask for reasons why they are discontented, combative, gossiping, and engaging in politicking. If there is anything you can do, work together on a plan with specific actionable items to find alignment to the team's mission and lift performance, plus a timeline to start seeing results. If satisfactory improvements are not made, the best option for everyone may be to part ways.

Productive Conflict and Conflict Resolution

Conflict, especially the unproductive kind, may be triggered by a variety of situations: a discussion that quickly gets out of hand, patterns of behavior that don't live up to expectations, and many other reasons. A challenge for managers is how to remediate such conflicts in a productive manner, maintain composure, and guide the conversation in a direction where it becomes positive and geared toward coming up with a solution or an agreement to seek a solution.

For most of us, it is natural that our first reaction is to avoid such conflicts and delay addressing them, wishfully thinking that if we wait long enough, they will go away. In reality, the longer we wait, the worse the situation becomes. Rather than postponing, work to address the conflict. This is never easy, which means preparation becomes paramount.

The preparation begins with you building an understanding of the root cause of the conflict, and that includes thinking about your contributions to it. Instead of trying to keep it all in your head, write down all the reasons you can think of (theirs and yours), plus topics you want to discuss. That will help you organize your thoughts and be as objective as possible. Then, work on identifying a good time to have a conversation—rarely is it the case that "now" is a good option. Next, refine your notes, which you read ahead of the conversation, then share them with the problematic person or other people you would like to invite to the conversation. Finally, schedule a meeting. Below is an example of notes that might form the basis of such a meeting:

> Blake,
>
> In our next one-on-one, I would like to spend some time talking about alignment to our team values, a few observed incidents by me, and feedback I have received from your colleagues. Please look at the following items. I would like to hear your perspective on those and understand where you are coming from.
>
> This is a friendly conversation where you should feel free and safe to speak. Once we listen and understand each other's points of view, we will be able to evaluate the situation with complete information:

- During the architectural design meeting last week, you were combative about everyone's opinions.
- In the same meeting, you rolled your eyes, making sure that the speaker noticed.
- Your on-call incident report mentioned several issues with systems we integrate with, but the resolution to the problem did not require modifications in any of those systems. Instead we had to deploy a new version of our system with a bug fix.
- During architectural design meetings, perhaps I should mediate discussions more actively.

Sample 4.7: Pre-Read Note.

In 1950, mathematician John Nash earned his PhD with a dissertation on noncooperative games. It defined the properties of the Nash Equilibrium and made the "Prisoner's Dilemma" its most famous example. The interaction dynamics take place because neither party has complete information and neither has the incentive to maximize their chances of winning while also minimizing the chances of the other party (zero-sum games). Later, in 1953, Nash published "Two-Person Cooperative Games," in which he shows that if the prisoners had freedom of communication and complete information, the dynamics of equilibrium would change and, rather than compete, they would cooperate.

Such conversations are difficult not only for you, but also for all parties involved. Commonly, the stakes are high, there are differences of opinion, and the outcomes can have a high impact. The first step to starting a productive dialogue is to establish a common purpose to address the root cause of the conflict.

Prepare the situation and circumstances before bringing up the topic of the conversation. Explain that this is a safe and respectful environment to talk. Make the people feel comfortable listening to you and understand that you will speak candidly and respectfully. Explain that they may share their own perspective without fear of being criticized or retaliated against. Once all parties feel safe to speak and listen, the conditions for gaining complete information are established, and the conversation becomes productive. Now you all have what is necessary for engaging in a dynamic of cooperation, rather than competition.

As perfect as circumstances may be, such conversations may cause people to overreact emotionally when topics that generate friction are brought up. Remain calm, and give the others some space to breathe with a small pause in the conversation. A few moments of silence will be beneficial. Remind the people of the meeting's purpose and that this is a safe environment. Then resume the conversation and avoid being sidetracked by anyone changing the subject. The purpose of the conversation is to address a point of conflict. Stick to it. That said, always be respectful, and expect the same in return. Everyone should speak candidly and respectfully.

It becomes ever more important to communicate with clarity and explain the purpose and context of the conversation. Many people, when having such conversations, inadvertently tend to use long, convoluted sentences; that is understandable, since it is uncomfortable for everyone to be in such a situation. This, however, may lead to even more discomfort due to misunderstanding. To avoid those circumstances, prepare yourself by, for instance, writing it down and rehearsing what you want to say. Speak clearly to facilitate understanding. As a rule of thumb, describe the gap between expectation and observation. Here is a hypothetical conversation in which a manager [you] insists on sticking to the subject:

> **You**: During the on-call incident you mentioned that systems were taking too long to respond.
>
> **Blake**: Yeah, the system we connect to is antiquated. Every time they say they will upgrade to a new version or implement push notification service they fall short on their promises. If the company was serious about it and refactored the system using a more modern language, we would have a much more reliable end point and faster responses.
>
> **You**: [Pause] Thank you for sharing, Blake. Can you help me understand the correlation between those improvements and our implementation of the fix?
>
> **Blake**: No, I was just saying that the system will work much better when they implement that.
>
> **You**: Indeed, it seems that the changes will make things much better. But for now, can we focus on the specifics of the on-call incident?
>
> **Blake**: Sure, no problem. The slowness was on our side because we were allocating a new data processor every time we received

a response. We implemented a pool of resources and are reusing instances whenever possible. Responses are fast in 99.9 percent of the cases now. We only need to allocate new instances very rarely.
You: Thanks, Blake. I appreciate your help understanding the core issue.

Sample 4.8: Sticking to the Topic.

At the same time, proper understanding of the message may take a while. Communicating clearly is not about short sentences. It is about continuity of thought and verifying that we understand each other. Everyone should be encouraged to repeat back to the speaker, in their own words, their understanding of what they heard. It may feel weird in the beginning, but it will prevent attrition later.

Another reaction you may observe in a conversation is someone coming up with perfectly good excuses to justify the conflict at hand. Those reactions are usually a variation of the Drama Triangle human interaction model proposed by Stephen Karpman. The model classifies actors as playing one or more of the following roles:

- **Persecutor**: Blames others and shows no accountability. Shows critical, controlling, and authoritarian behavior.
- **Rescuer**: Acts to save the day. Wants to be recognized. Ignores their own responsibilities under the excuse of helping others.
- **Victim**: Believes there was nothing that could be done. Feels helpless, oppressed, and unable to act.

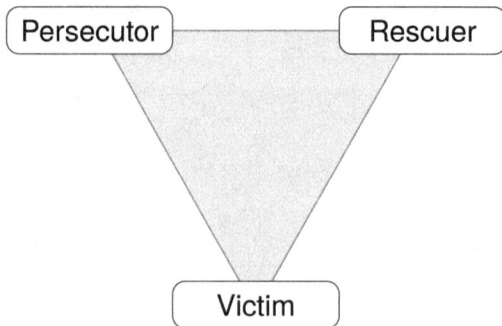

Figure 4.6: Drama Triangle.

Surprisingly, people are seldom aware that they are acting as one or more of those protagonists. The most observed behavior is the "victim," who often alleviates and dodges responsibility through blaming others. Whatever the case, there is a good chance that conflict has arisen because of the excuses from the drama triangle, not despite them.

Conclude the conversation with a set of clear, actionable items for all applicable parties. Write down the expectations for everyone's account-ability, and share them via an online document that is accessible to all involved. This will be important to ensure progress and resolution. The expectations should have the what and the how. Avoid being too rigid regarding the actionable items. Have some flexibility if there is some progress being made in the right direction. Here is an example of a list of actionable items:

> Blake,
> Thank you for the conversation. I appreciate your trusting me to speak candidly.
>
> Here are the topics we agreed to act upon over the next few weeks:
> - If I notice that you have become combative during meetings, I will message you privately letting you know. This way, you can become aware of the behavior and adjust it accordingly. The expectation is that such behavior will disappear over the next three months.
> - Reporting from on-call incidents should contain only descriptions of issues and fixes directly related to the incident.

Sample 4.9: Actionable Items.

As challenging and uncomfortable as such conflicts may feel in the begin-ning, after those conversations take place and the issues are resolved, you may end up with better professional relationships and reinforced trust in each other.

Career Framework

Projects will grow in features and number of products, and people will develop subject matter expertise and improve their capabilities to work on more complex assignments. At the same time, discuss with team members their view of options for a career path. One common way to add transparency is to publish a framework that describes the various professional levels and the requirements, skills, and capabilities expected within job families. This way, the team will have a clear understanding of where focus and effort are needed for their career progress. The intention of the framework, however, is not to be a to-do list one must complete before one is automatically promoted. Instead, the framework is a document intended to provide guidance for everyone's career path.

With a framework in their hands, people can accept accountability for their own career progress and work with you, the manager, to develop themselves in areas where they see the need for improvement or areas where they already perform well and want to grow stronger. Since you will learn more about their professional growth aspirations, include those as topics to talk about in one-on-one conversations to encourage and support their development.

Creating this document is a task you should complete in collaboration with your human resources colleague. That person will know policy requirements, current terminology, and other details pertinent to the career path.

There are three fundamental pillars that define and support a good career framework:

1. Define the career levels. Whether the person is an individual contributor or a people leader, what is the entry level? How many levels? What is the current highest level? (More levels can be added later as people progress in their careers.)
2. Within each level, describe the necessary skills, nice-to-have skills, performance expectations, networking capabilities, and other items you think are necessary. Be careful to include only what is absolutely needed. A lengthy list of items may be discouraging and unrealistic. Less is better.
3. Ensure the document is easily searchable and accessible to everyone on the team. Publish it in the company's knowledge base, include a link from the team's shared drive, bring it up periodically in meetings, and share it with all new team

members. Make sure that everyone is aware of it, knows where to find it, and that they can request a copy from you or HR.

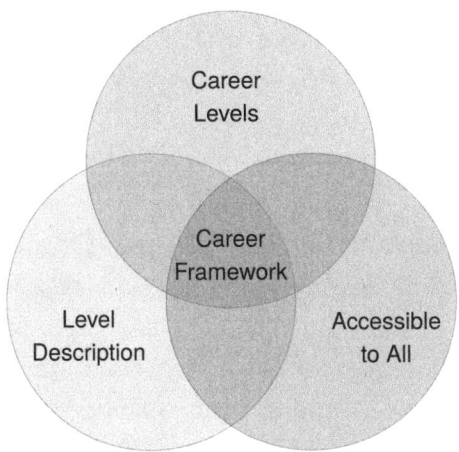

Figure 4.7: Fundamental Pillars of a Career Framework.

There is an element of transparency that is not immediately apparent in career frameworks. By being clear about requirements, skill, expectations, and more, it promotes more growth opportunities for all employees, thus becoming an effective instrument for leveling the playing field, allowing for all employees, without giving preference to any specific group.

Individual Contributor		People Leader
Engineering	**Research**	**Management**
		M4—Director
	R4—Principal	M3—Sr Manager
T4—Principal	R3—Sr Researcher	M2—Manager
T3—Sr Engineer	R2—Researcher	M1—Associate
T2—Engineer	R1—Associate	
T1 – Associate		

Table 4.3: Career Framework Levels.

Table 4.3 shows a simple example of defining career levels. It contains the paths for both individual contributors and people leaders.

The next step is to describe each level. For the sake of brevity, the example shown in Sample 4.8, below picks one level from each of the career level verticals, otherwise it would become too verbose. The sample presented here is enough for you to understand the central idea and adapt it for your own cases.

Career Level	Skills Description
T2—Engineer	Engineering establishes the *how* a feature or product will be implemented, from understanding the requirements and translating specifications into sound system architecture, to the choices of programming languages, frameworks, service providers, and so on. Stability and quality of the system are also top of mind. Since inception, reliability, observability, and criteria for testing should be part of the design. Longevity and maintainability are important factors, too. Producing well-written documentation and hosting knowledge transfer sessions are great ways to disseminate know-how among engineers. • Demonstrated experience with the development of software in real-life products. • Verifiable experience with an object-oriented language. • Great communication and interpersonal skills. • Basic experience with Agile methodologies. • Code review feedback that is seen by teammates as a significant improvement.
R3—Sr. Researcher	Senior research discovers what is possible with data, systems, and technology in general. New trends, tools, frameworks, data insights, techniques for modeling, and more. They are trailblazers and harbingers. Mechanisms for transitioning from the current state to the next is a constant on the radar. Adopting the future should be a smooth process that either gives continuity or replaces existing solutions.

	• Ability to take initiative and the determination to turn data into real-life insights. • Ability to tackle problems related to scalability, performance, and observability of systems. • Excellent communication skills, both written and verbal. • Active and influential contributor in the design of systems and services. • Experience collaborating with product managers understanding business requirements.
M2—Manager	Management is about being effective in a variety of domains. From the well-being and professional growth of the team to communication, to delivering products, and more. Typically, with a strong technical background, managers actively take part in all four streams. Autonomy and responsibility are fundamental attributes. • Ability to host conversations with the team, fostering an environment where communication flows. • Record of encouraging the team to have ownership of tasks and autonomy to act. • Collaboration with product managers to advance engineering and product hand in hand. • Excellent communication skills, both written and verbal. • Fluency with Agile methodologies. • Frequent updates upstream regarding the status of projects, challenges, and asks. • Demonstrable experience collaborating with product managers specifying business requirements.

Sample 4.10: Career Framework Description of Skills.

Planning resources and respective allocations become easier with a career framework like the one shown on Sample 4.8. You will be better informed about the roles you have, where to hire, and which talent you need to grow. Can you fill the gaps with existing team members? Who has the potential to step up and fill those gaps? Do you need to hire someone from outside the company?

In case someone leaves the team, a career framework will be useful in writing the profile of the candidate you will need to hire to replace the person departing. Note here that there are two possible scenarios. First, you hire someone new, who is either an outsider or a transfer from another team. Second, someone from the team takes the vacated role, and you will hire a new "backfill" employee "with the qualifications and the skill set of the [departing] one to fill the vacancy for a given period of time . . . to ensure continuity," which takes you back to the first scenario.

Since the career framework is published in the company's knowledge base and is accessible to all, being better informed becomes a two-way street. There is a positive effect on engagement and retention because everyone can compare their professional growth against it and verify whether there is alignment. At a minimum, there is an understanding of fairness given to their careers. They will either be engaged and committed, or they will identify misalignment early on and look for a better fit elsewhere. In either case, the outcome is favorable to all.

Guidance is another attribute of a career framework. It goes without saying that there are expectations that employees will be improving skills and growing capabilities, but sometimes it is hard to know where to start. A career framework can be seen as a blueprint of where to focus for professional growth.

Grading

Evaluating the performance of your team is a high-impact task in the sense that it will affect the lives of the people on the team, your ability to execute how projects are implemented, and the success of products and the company.

Broadly speaking, there are three grades for members of your team: High performer, delivering, and low performer. At first, this classification may appear to be oversimplistic, but this is not the case since there are multiple characteristics, a.k.a. dimensions, you will be evaluating to determine the overall category. These include technical competency, communication effectiveness, contributions, networking, and more. A person may show great technical competency and fall short in effective communication. But how can you measure, represent, understand, and explain a multidimensional hypercube? This apparently simple construct is necessary for comprehension and explainability. When you must fill out a form and are asked to select a box from a small set, even though you know that there are other possible options, that set was by design and necessity, not by accident.

Many companies adopt the nine-box calibration tool developed by McKinsey & Company, where a two-dimensional plane is used to evaluate people. The person's "performance" is on the x-axis and "potential" is on the y-axis. Even this system can be simplified into three grades with zones in red, yellow, and green, or different shades of gray.

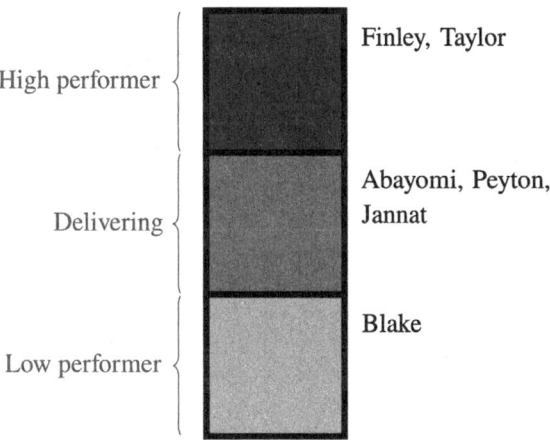

Figure 4.8: Grading Scale.

I prefer the simplicity, objectivity, and understandability of the three grades, as shown in Figure 4.8 with the names of the team members next to their respective classifications.

Having many boxes to choose from will not only produce a mass of scattered points but also reduce anyone's ability to understand what they mean. Less is more in this case.

The performance of a team member is not an absolute and immutable classification that stays unchanged. It is variable over time. Most people go through moments of higher or lower performance, and there are many reasons for that fluctuation. A previously high performer may now be taking care of a newborn or is dealing with a family issue. An otherwise low performer may have finished their PhD thesis and now has more time and energy to focus and dedicate themselves to hard work. The list goes on. The important part is to understand that there will be oscillations from the baseline, and these variations should be considered.

Usually these variations are moderate, rather than the high ups and low downs of a roller coaster. High variability comes with its own set of issues, with the most impact on a sustainable productivity velocity.

You are right in assuming that the diagram in Figure 4.8 is insufficient to satisfy the conditions for an objective grading. As pointed out, there are several dimensions being evaluated. To be fair to the company, to the project, to the team, and to each person, you need to complement the diagram with a formalized written evaluation for each of the dimensions used to classify a team member.

I recommend that you write it down; when you translate your thoughts into words in a document, you are minimizing the chances of introducing bias. Your thinking needs to be structured and cohesive; rereading your own words will give you the chance to determine fairness. A project is a measure of success for the company and the team. Team members want to work with other great players, and each person wants to feel confident that their evaluation will help them grow professionally and is not arbitrary. The writing will give you the conviction and peace of mind to support the grading.

The following is a sample written evaluation for each dimension used to classify each team member.

Technical competency and contributions

- **Finley**: The infrastructure is deployed and maintained by Finley. The new dashboard is also a great example of technical ability and technical leadership since Finley mentored ours and other teams in adopting the new tool. When asked, Finley can learn new things quickly, but it may take some convincing.
- **Taylor**: The introduction of the health check APIs made a profound impact in our ability to monitor the availability of the systems and to be able to act quickly in the event of an outage. Taylor could be more proactive in meetings, rather than waiting to be asked for input.
- **Abayomi**: Contributions are not limited to one project. Abayomi actively took part in the implementation and release

of *Project A* and was a key contributor integrating *Project B* with the APIs for security diagnosing.

- **Peyton**: The new interactive widgets in the dashboard are a direct contribution from Peyton. In addition, Peyton is the scrum master for the team and most recently took a mentorship role to onboarding new hires. Peyton needs frequent checks on progress being made at work. If left alone, Peyton lacks the tenacity to keep the momentum going.
- **Jannat**: Refactoring of the user interface to use the new paradigms of the programming language allows for much quicker prototyping and A/B testing of features to be released to users. Jannat could be a little more patient when interacting with back-end engineers asking for new APIs and expectation of completion.
- **Blake**: The potential is there, and Blake knows how to make contributions. However, Blake often chooses simple tasks and takes longer than expected to complete them. Furthermore, Blake often takes conversations into "what-if" scenarios that don't have an impact on the development of the product.

Networking and communications
- **Finley**: Having been with the company for several years, Finley is very well connected across teams and often exchanges ideas, experiences, and solicits advice. Finley's network goes beyond the project and includes ML, mobile, back end, front end, and beyond.
- **Abayomi**: People often reach out to Abayomi in search of advice, mentorship, etc. Abayomi is well connected within technology. A new challenge would be to start building connections in the Product, Marketing, and Sales teams.
- **Taylor**: Has good connections, but it is limited to the scope of the project and related activities. It would be good to see Taylor build a wider network.
- **Peyton**: Well-connected and takes the initiative to reach out and network with workmates when needed. Peyton is also a

prolific writer and often publishes technical articles on the company's blog.

- **Jannat**: Frequent speaker at meetings and shares valuable insights. Jannat expresses thoughts with clarity and simplicity, making it easy for listeners to follow the point in question. Having joined the company less than a year ago, Jannat is still developing connections outside the technical team.
- **Blake**: Great communicator but seems to be more focused on speaking at conferences than in meetings and technical discussions. There are also problems with situations where an agreement is reached about an implementation; rather than committing, Blake tries to reopen the conversation time and again.

Sample 4.11: Grading Write-Down.

This exercise in grading will, in large part, be used as a foundation to determine promotions, compensation calculations, career path, team composition (retention or potentially removal of a low performer), and other places where it may be useful.

Letting People Go

In the "Grading" section, we saw an objective and fair way to classify members of the team. In this section, we will focus on people who were consistently graded as low performers. There is no rule of thumb since each case needs to be analyzed individually and with proper context. One is not immediately let go if classified as a low performer. It might be that the person is just not a good fit for the job or team; when the person was hired, someone saw potential in them.

However understanding you may be, there is the challenge of weighing your ability to accommodate a person's circumstances versus the responsibilities to the project. How long and how much impact are acceptable? In addition to all we have discussed so far, consider that there is an invisible perverse incentive at play such that the other members of the team are aware of at least part of the situation. Based on what they have observed, they may become less motivated to perform well because person X does not perform well and gets away with it.

Why should they be the ones to work hard? They ask how this situation is fair to them.

If the person committed an unforgivable transgression, is a constant low performer, or has a competency problem, the best option may be to let the person go and help them find an opportunity where they would be a better fit. Where the situation is not clear—there could be many reasons why the person is underperforming—bring up your concerns in a one-on-one meeting, and give the person a chance to explain the reason behind their lackluster performance. During the conversation, present clear examples of where you have concerns, and follow up with a written message reiterating the items covered during the meeting and your expectation for areas of improvement. Sample 4.10 is an example of such message:

Blake,

Following our last conversation, I wanted to reiterate the feedback we discussed so that we have a reference document. My expectations for you and the other members of the team reflect a high degree of autonomy, systems thinking, engineering craftsmanship, and communication. In line with this, there are important areas for improvement that I would like you to focus on in the coming weeks:

- The rate at which progress is made in line with your objectives.
- The volume and quality of your contributions to the codebase.
- Clear articulations of your findings and engineering objectives.
- A decrease in the perception by your teammates—and me—regarding your productivity. You have fewer and less significant contributions compared to your teammates.

To make this feedback as concrete as possible I would like to outline some examples:

1. A couple of weeks back, during a 1:1, you mentioned that your teammates think they may not be able to trust you to complete tasks.
2. During this quarter, your work on implementing minimum quality tests of newly trained ML models took quite a long

time to complete, significantly more time than similar past implementations.

3. Reviewing your contributions to the codebase, the frequency and number of contributions is much less when compared to other engineers on the team.

4. During the last retrospective meeting, you posed a series of what-if scenarios about the model-UI interaction that were a distraction to the team and did not add to the conversation. Afterward, I received feedback from others, who expressed some frustration. This is one example, but there have been other similar episodes.

This letter is to share with you what is holding you back and to give you the information you need to improve. It is my responsibility and part of my job to make you aware, so we can both work on addressing those items. Meeting these expectations is essential to your success, and I would be doing you a disservice if I were to be vague. I look forward to seeing improvement in these areas and to periodically revisiting this conversation to evaluate progress.

I am always available to discuss these or any other matters and am committed to your success.

Thank you,
[Your name]

Sample 4.12: Follow-up Message.

In addition to sending the message to that individual, forward a copy of it to your HR person, who should already be aware of the performance concerns you have about this member of your team. HR is your ally and can guide you through the process.

Depending on how your company operates, a performance improvement plan, or PIP, may be the next step. If the person did not show improvement and did not meet the expectations set out in the conversation and follow-up message, then you need to adopt a more formal process. You must do this together with your HR counterpart, which is another reason why HR needs to be aware of the situation from the beginning.

There are cases where people respond positively to the feedback, match PIP expectations, and can improve their performance. It is great when this happens. That, however, is not the end of the conversation. You still need to clearly communicate that you expect them, at a minimum, to maintain that level of performance. It would not be acceptable to be in a situation where, in the future, the same problems come up again, leading to a vicious cycle of performance improvement, backsliding, then a return to improvement. You get the picture.

The last stage is when the person in question cannot or did not want to meet the expectations you spelled out. Continue working with your HR representative to facilitate the offboarding process. As far as possible, try to help the person with details about the severance package, contacts with recruiters, and a plan for knowledge-transfer sessions, if applicable.

A person can be let go because they were not a good fit for the job and keep their dignity at the same time. Being unfit for a job does not mean the person is an incompetent professional. For instance, Lee Iacocca, who helped create the Ford Mustang, was once fired for having a different mindset from the company's CEO. He went on to become the CEO of Chrysler, where he rescued the company from near bankruptcy and transformed the auto industry of his time. While other members of the team may be curious to know what transpired, you should let the person who is leaving decide whether to disclose details.

Promotions

When you plan to promote someone, you want them to continue being successful in their career. Before moving forward with a recommendation for promotion, begin by progressively assigning next-level tasks to that person. This will prepare them to be successful in their new role and will also give you a sense of their readiness for it. For instance, ask a T2 engineer (one step above entry-level engineer) to propose a design for a part of the system, and present the design to the team.

Promotions are merit-based and earned. They are not given by tenure nor by checking the boxes of a career framework. Promotions are for those who are actively and deliberately pursuing the next level in their careers and have demonstrable results to show their effectiveness. It does not matter how long the person has been in that position.

There are cases where people find their comfort zone and just cruise along. There are also times when you are pressured to promote someone because they came to you directly and asked for a promotion. In both cases, what message would you be sending to the team? In the former, is it acceptable to go along for the ride and be rewarded with a promotion? In the latter, does it mean that when someone asks you to promote someone and you agree, you are showing preferential treatment? How is either scenario fair to the team? These are delicate situations.

In the first scenario, a person may be studying at night to obtain a new degree, going through a family problem, or struggling with professional ambitions. All those are possible reasons for someone to be productive, make significant contributions to projects, yet not be purposely trying to advance in their careers. In the second scenario, the person may be ready for and deserving of a promotion. However, if you decide to promote them, it must be a merit-based decision, not because you were asked. These are valuable team members, and if you think long enough, you must come up with a justifiable reason to promote them.

How do you promote with objective criteria? The answer is to build a portfolio with information and evaluations about the person and write down the justification for a promotion. When you put words to a document, your thoughts are structured, your arguments are concise, and you can work on it over time. In short, it becomes a legitimate process. Otherwise, you run the risk of upsetting and even losing team members; high performers will be the first to go.

The portfolio should have, among other things, the title change, a mini bio, a summary of the proposal, a list of accomplishments, and references from colleagues. In addition to being fair to the other teammates, the document will be fair to the person being recommended for promotion. As the proposal reaches other approvers upstream, they may not be familiar with the person's work or lack information. The document will provide more context and increase the odds that the request for promotion is approved. In essence, you would be telling a story and supporting it with evidence.

Work on the document with the person being recommended for promotion. It should not be a task you do by yourself. The person will play an active role in contributing content, editing, and reviewing. One special section is references. Ask the person to pick two or three people to write them a recommendation. Irrespective of who collects the quotes, make sure you directly contact the people who wrote them and get their permission to use their words in the document.

Finley
From: T2—Engineer
To: T3—Sr Engineer

Mini Bio
Finley is a former amusement park mechanic turned back end engineer, with particular interest in message passing in distributed systems. A person with the determination to do what needs to be done to complete a project, Finley is happiest when a project is shipped and in the hands of customers using it. Current contributions include the multicloud platform and the high-availability systems. Books are a constant companion, from thrillers to technical, in audio, print, or electronic format. Some say that Finley's books are like a backup to the local library.

Summary Case
Since joining the company, Finley has made significant contributions to numerous projects and teams, notably coming up with the solution for distributed database writes.
- Spearheaded product-oriented overhaul of distributed systems, proposing using single-queue message passing for lock-free writing to the distributed database.
- Helped determine key causes for high latency (delay in network communications) and proposed changes to speed up the streaming service, making for more responsive user experience.
- Contributed engineering expertise, code, and reviews required for producing a working implementation of the product, now released into production.

Accomplishments
- Deployed the distributed system to production
- Made numerous contributions to the codebase
  https://repository-A
  https://repository-n
- Contributed to the knowledge base
  https://article-A
  https://article-n
- Organized and hosted a technology book club to foster engineering excellence

References

Jaden, Principal Engineer

"Finley really embodies craftsmanship in engineering. I get the sense that given a specific business problem, Finley will know what engineering approach will work and what will not. This combination of confidence, experience, and pragmatism is super-powerful when it comes to getting stuff done. Finley is a sharp professional and a good listener who has plenty of ideas. (We welcome ideas!!) If I were embarking on a back-end engineering project, I'd ask for Finley."

Rae, Product Manager

"I had the opportunity to work with Finley on the 'Anatomical Aardvark' project and was impressed by his suggestions of solutions that captured the needs of customers and engineering. Finley was knowledgeable and a pleasure to work with. I have witnessed Finley's willingness to step up whenever there were issues raised by customers during the development phase. There was always a prompt response, help to triage the issue, and advice on the next steps. Finley is a great collaborator and solutions-oriented professional."

Sample 4.13: Promotion Profile.

When everything is ready, submit the recommendation for the promotion and include the portfolio document. Although there are no guarantees that it will be approved by upstream managers, the likelihood will be higher since they will have proper context.

Broadly speaking, there are three possible outcomes for the promotion proposal:

- It is declined. There may be many reasons for that, including but not limited to, unavailable head count, financial budget, near-term organizational restructuring, and more. Whatever the reason, if it is not related to the person being recommended for promotion, try again later. If it is about the person, find out what the shortcomings are, work to improve in those areas, and retry.
- It is postponed. There is an understanding from upstream management that the case is a good one and that it should happen, but for one reason or another, it is not possible to approve it now. You can ask for a tentative timeline and follow up as the deadline approaches.
- It is acccpted. Time to celebrate.

Whatever the outcome, schedule a meeting with the person, share the news, and discuss next steps.

Assuming that the promotion was approved, recognize the work, dedication, and determination the employee put in to earn it. The focus should be on acknowledging the merit. Although a celebration, the circumstances are different from winning a raffle, where little to no effort is required. Explain how and when it will take place, changes in the job title, compensation, organizational structure, and other relevant information.

On the day the promotion takes place, announce it to the rest of the team both verbally and in a written message. You want them to see this as an example for themselves, to look up to the person being promoted, and to learn that if they want to grow professionally and be promoted, they can follow some of the same or similar steps as their newly promoted teammate. Then invite everyone to celebrate.

Quality of Life

Much has been said and written about achieving work-life balance. How can someone maintain a good quality of life while making meaningful contributions at work and feeling like a productive person?

Before we continue, let me make a distinction between two kinds of companies, then develop the topic separately for each of them.

1. Early-stage startups or companies facing an existential risk.
2. All other companies.

The way to interpret quality of life depends on context. If a company has just begun and is trying to find its place in the world, or if an existing company is under existential threat and may close its doors, quality of life is less about finding work-life balance and more about working hard to reach escape velocity and build a better future. Only when the company finds itself in a more comfortable position can you look for a more stable routine with separation between work and homelife.

This phase of high-intensity work is not sustainable in the long run. There are exceptions (e.g., Elon Musk, some startup founders), but I am not aware of many employees who can work long hours, most days, for many years. At some point, most people burn out if equilibrium is lacking.

When talking about all other companies, quality of life begins with people leaders creating the necessary circumstances for it to happen. Telling people to take time off and go on vacation to an exotic destination will change nothing and make little to no difference. Yes, people enjoy vacations, but as the name implies, that is time away from the office. Work-life balance is for all those other times when people are involved in the normal routines of life; in other words, most of their time.

Deadlines, deliverables, and commitments are always there, and people become reluctant to working anything short of 24/7. There is an invisible pressure to demonstrate that they are the ones who work harder and longer, and sacrifice everything to get something done, only to burn out a while later and leave the company for a perceived better job elsewhere.

Messages—emails, instant messages, and other forms of communication—are sent, depending on the company, all day long, early morning to late at night and during off-hours. There is an implicit expectation that the person on the receiving end will reply, and that person may fear consequences if they don't. They may wonder if people will think they are not contributing enough or are not a team player. Inevitably, everyone is caught in this vicious cycle, and some are even unaware that it is happening. It is easy to see that the cost of such dynamics is overworked and unhappy people.

Yes, there are times when it is necessary to work long hours and weekends, and to reply to messages late at night, during moments of critical importance, or in the case of an emergency. Although these are a reality, they should not be the norm. Preferably, they are few and far between.

The situation with unrelenting messages described here is one, among many factors in attaining work-life balance, and in my experience, it is perhaps the single largest contributor to the imbalance. Creating the circumstances for a better quality of life begins with the leadership team. You, as the manager, are the one who must establish the terms of engagement. It can be surprisingly simple to establish such terms, only requiring you to periodically revisit them then checking with the team to confirm the dynamics are operating as intended. You may ask, "What can the manager do?"

Start by establishing core hours for communication. This is irrespective of a team being distributed across several different time zones or all located in the same office. Each person has their own core hours when they will be working. In the United States, typical office hours are from 9:00 a.m. to 5:00 p.m. During a person's working hours, they are expected to join meetings, reply to messages, and do other tasks related to their job.

During off-hours, employees are not expected to participate in any of those activities, unless told that there is a critical situation or an emergency. At such times, an all-hands-on-deck effort may be necessary.

For a person sending a message, they may not know the recipient's core working hours or what needs to be communicated. It is best to send the message right away while it is still top of mind. It is perfectly fine for a person to send a message at any time. It is also perfectly fine for the receiving party not to reply to that message during nonworking hours—unless there is an emergency. All parties understand that if there is no expectation to interact nor to receive a response, the message can wait until the next day. Most important, you, the manager, should be aware and supportive of this dynamic. With your support to implement this fundamental operational rule, team members need not feel guilty about waiting to respond the next day. On the other hand, if you are not supportive, employees might feel pressured to respond to work-related messages early or late—at the expense of their personal time—out of fear they won't be perceived as team players.

This is not meant as a prohibition against people responding to messages during nonworking hours nor is it an excuse to evade responsibility. It is fine for people to reply to noncritical messages during off-hours. To preserve a decent quality of life, though, there should be zero expectations to do so. It should be an employee's choice to reply or not.

If a message begins with a keyword such as Urgent, Critical, or Emergency, that signals that this is a situation that requires their immediate attention, which is sometimes the reality of operations. Messages without such key words can wait until working hours. Some senders may even add courtesy keywords indicating that a message can wait, for example, Not Urgent.

How employees manage time in their personal life is up to them. Part of our job as leaders is to create the circumstances where they can separate work and personal time in a way that is sustainable in the long run. There will be a lot less burnout, and people will be more productive during their working hours.

Have Fun

Activities at work include more than transactional laboring to complete tasks. Humans are social animals and need interactions, even in the professional context, that are unstructured and unrelated to day-to-day in-person or remote work.

Informal water cooler–type conversations are part of the workplace culture, irrespective of the size of the company. At a small startup, a Fortune 500 corporation, or somewhere in between, people always engage in casual conversation. This speaks to our need to socialize, whether someone is an introvert or an extrovert.

In addition to these informal, unplanned moments, there is room for being intentional about having fun, notably in group activities unrelated to work. Everyone or just a few on the team may want to join in. It should be completely up to them.

In tech-related work, hackathons are often popular. Anyone can take part, form teams, and hack with others to try out an idea. The idea itself may be related, unrelated, or tangential to projects at work. The important thing is people are working together to build something. At the end of the activity, perhaps have independent judges grade the results. If there are judges, there must also be a prize, which could be something small, symbolic, and fun. One note: check with the legal team first about company policy for such prizes because there may be strict limits for items that could be considered a gift.

Informal chats can also be fun. Structured one-on-one meetings are typically focused on your direct reports. How about less formal two-on-one or three-on-one chats? Those can be fun and related to topics outside work, such as books, hobbies, adventures, and much more. It is a great way for people to get to know each other better, and friendly familiarity can lead to bonding, which is healthy for teams. Plan those occasions. Block the time on your calendar, send an invite, and get together for a walk, a chat at the coffee shop, a Ping-Pong match, or a board game. Whatever works for your team, make it happen.

Before you organize an activity and invite everyone to join, invest some time into getting to know what events or activities interest your team members. Learn what they consider fun. After all, you, the manager, may love something, but the team may consider it boring, or worse, they may feel like they're doing the adult version of kindergarten activities.

Even more unfortunate is when an activity is organized by a well-meaning but over-enthusiastic and uninformed event organizer. You may end up with an invitation to jump blindfolded from an airplane into an active volcano to do hot yoga and eat lava-roasted marshmallows. Seriously, it is better to give the team a day off than to compel them to participate in something they will neither enjoy nor appreciate.

Here are a few activities that I have done with my teams over the years. Some may appeal to you: hiking an easy to moderate trail, go-kart racing, ice-skating, watching a game at the ballpark, trying to escape from an escape room, visiting a national park, playing online games, sharing a meal at a restaurant, bowling, volunteering, and more.

Those moments create opportunities for people to talk, understand each other better, develop rapport, and engrain that sense of belonging discussed in Maslow's hierarchy of needs.

Sometimes crossing an important milestone is reason enough to celebrate by doing something fun. Shipping the first version of a product, releasing a customer-requested feature that everyone has been working hard to complete, and similar situations could inspire a celebratory event. Take a few moments to address the team and reflect on memories of the journey, obstacles that were overcome, and the satisfaction of accomplishment.

Sports teams celebrate when they win a championship. Your team should, too! Give shout-outs to those team members who went above and beyond to get the job done. Recognize that what they did made a difference. Let them express sincere pride in their accomplishment.

There should be an understanding that those fun events are not an entitlement nor a perk of the job. They are a special treat, a chance to get together and do something outside of work that everyone would enjoy.

To learn how to fund an activity, work with the head of your division or your counterparts in finance. Most companies have a small budget for fun events.

A word of caution, though. Be aware that all those activities must be governed by a code of conduct. Participants are required to behave in a civilized manner and be respectful of one another. Given that you are their people leader, excesses or inappropriate behavior may end with you and others being called in for an uncomfortable conversation with HR, legal, or both—and the consequences could be serious. Still, don't let this risk dissuade you from organizing fun group outings for your team. Talk candidly to the team about expected proper behavior. The object is to have good, clean fun. Consider the alternative and remember: The price of boredom is higher than the risks of fun.

CHAPTER 5

Managing Downstream: Project

One accurate measurement is worth a thousand expert opinions.
—Grace Hopper

Richard Feynman, corecipient of the 1965 Nobel Prize in Physics, pondered what foundational scientific statement would contain the most information in the least number of words, in the unlikely event human knowledge was destroyed and only a sentence could be passed on to the next generation.

His answer, found in *The Feynman Lectures on Physics*, spoke to the fundamental building blocks of matter: atoms.

> If we were to name the most powerful assumption of all, which leads one on and on in an attempt to understand life, it is that all things are made of atoms, and that everything that living things do can be understood in terms of the jigglings and wigglings of atoms.

Although there are more fundamental parts than atoms (e.g., electrons, protons, quarks), for the purposes of the analogy here, atoms are the basic building blocks, like Lego bricks. When used as an instruction set and assembled, atoms form molecules, which in turn form the universe we know.

It is this way, too, with products, which are conceptualized and assembled from smaller parts. Engineers use instructions in programming languages, transistors, networks, and more to put together the many components of a product. In management, the equivalent of those components are tasks, timelines, resources, and so forth, which are then combined in projects that abstractly represent the "chemical" reactions to the creation of products.

Before projects can be managed, we must recognize their fundamental components in the framework of tasks, timelines, and resources. There is a finite number of features and a finite amount of time in which to complete them. All projects have a life cycle. There are projects that may be long-lived and give the impression that there is an "infinite" number of features. Even in such projects, it is necessary to complete versions. For example, an automobile is an incredibly complex piece of engineering, yet many carmakers release new models every year.

Managing a project involves planning and defining features, limiting the scope of what is to be implemented, establishing deadlines, communicating responsibilities, demonstrating the results periodically to assess alignment between plan and implementation, and adjusting course when and where needed.

Planning

Chances are that you and your company already have a tool to help you manage projects. If not, there are many great options available. Find the one that works best for you, and start using it. Project management software provides a place where you can see the whole, measure progress against a timeline, gauge execution against planning, and utilize functions as an instrument that alerts you when development is at risk and allows you to act early. It is not uncommon for lower-priority tasks to show up unannounced, important tasks to take longer than originally estimated, and the scope of requirements to increase (a.k.a. scope creep).

When entering each ticket in the system, pay close attention to the three main elements of a task: *what, who,* and *when.* There are other elements to consider, such as links between tasks and the cost of implementation (usually using Fibonacci numbers 1, 2, 3, 5, 8, 13, 21, and so on), but the absolutely essential ones are those three elements. Figure 5.1 shows an example of a simple ticket with the core items.

Summary:

Data Extract API Specification.

Description:

Specify the endpoint, method, parameters, and data structure for the API to extract data and apply the transformation so it can be used in the processing pipeline.

Acceptance Criteria:

   - Secure endpoint only accepting a POST method.

   - Strongly typed input and output data structures expressed in protobuf.

   - Performance and integration tests.

   - Documentation of the API in the knowledge base.

Assignee:

Abayomi

Due:

Jun 1st

Figure 5.1: Example of a Planning Ticket.

The *what* defines what needs to be done, including the acceptance criteria used to define when it can be considered implemented. The description should be clear, rather than vague or ambivalent. Including diagrams and links to documents containing specifications are welcome additions. Equally important is delineating the criteria for acknowledging completion of the task.

The *who* specifies the person responsible for implementing the task. If not clear at the moment of creation, it is customary practice to assign the ticket to the product manager. Later, during a planning session, it is reassigned to the appropriate teammate.

Finally, the *when* establishes a deadline by which the task is expected to be complete. Pay special attention here. A date estimate does not bend space and time; unpredictable events might happen to delay completion. Maintain a balance of staying committed to the date, but also be understanding of unknowns. Ask your team to do their best to estimate with accuracy and adjust planning periodically. If your system does not have a due date field, it can be implicitly defined as the end of the assigned sprint. If the task spans multiple sprints, break it down into Part 1, Part 2, Part n. To the extent possible, you want to avoid last-minute surprises, both good and bad. If the team underpromises and overdelivers or the other way around, it means that planning could have been better. If the former is the case, the plan could have been more aggressive; if the latter applies, pressure to deliver may be too much, potentially impoverishing product quality.

One can make a case for assigning points to a task as an essential element. That is true when you adopt a quantitative approach and want to measure productivity velocity V and the impact of interruptions, as we saw previously in chapter 4 when discussing sustainable productivity velocity.

I like to think of the use of this point system as a scale analogous to climbing flights of stairs. They are not necessarily related to time, although they take time. Instead, they represent the estimated effort required to complete a task. Climbing one flight of stairs is relatively easy, assuming one is a healthy person with no physical disabilities. Climbing two flights of stairs requires a little more effort, but one can do it without much effort. It will become progressively harder and harder to climb 3, 5, 8, 13, and sequentially more flights of stairs. The person climbing may need to stop to catch their breath and rest their legs. The same concept can be applied to tasks in a sprint. A simple task A may be assigned one or two points and a complex one B perhaps eight or thirteen points. One may not know how long it will take to complete either task, but the understanding is clear that effort B is greater than effort A.

Prioritizing

Circumstances are always changing, and the prioritization of tasks on the plan should reflect that and adapt to new knowledge, requirements, understandings, and more. The change here is incremental, where the team may be considering a small refactoring of the code, changes in the user interface, the adoption of a new tool, or upgrading the version of a dependency. Should the changes be material enough, that may require reevaluating the project and perhaps even pivoting.

Every week or two the team should gather to discuss the contents of the backlog, reevaluate the need for existing tasks, add new tasks as needed, and prioritize the order of execution. A good practice for prioritizing backlog items is to draw a 2D chart with four quadrants, commonly known as an Eisenhower matrix or urgent-important matrix. The horizontal axis represents the urgency; the vertical axis represents the importance. The farthest up and to the right from the origin, the more important and urgent the task is; the farthest down and to the left of the origin, the less important and urgent.

The upper-right quadrant contains the tasks that are both important and urgent, and that is where the team should focus. The bottom-left quadrant contains the tasks that are not important and not urgent; it is an easy decision to avoid focusing there. The other two quadrants, however, are the most challenging, and this is where there is the most difficulty in finding an alignment of priorities among team members. The top left contains tasks that are important, but not urgent, and the bottom right contains tasks that are urgent, but not important.

Once you complete the tasks that are both important and urgent, a question naturally arises: Which tasks should the team focus on next? Should the team work on the tasks that are important but not urgent? Or should the team work on the tasks that are urgent? The answer may surprise you: neither. The best thing to do is to reprioritize the backlog and, given the new context, identify which tasks are both important and urgent.

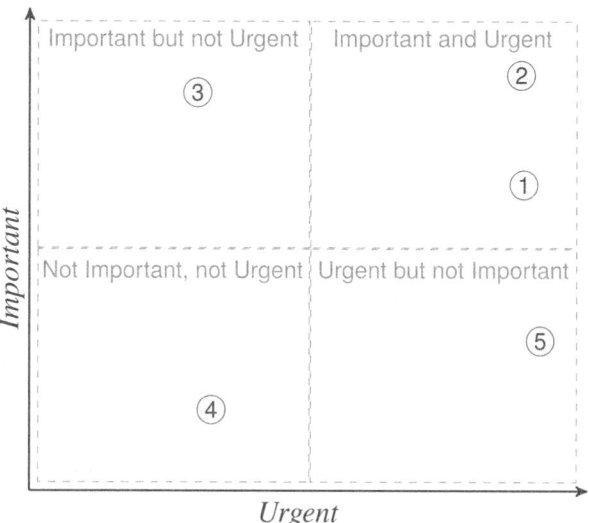

Figure 5.2: Important vs. Urgent.

In Figure 5.2, we can see that the focus should be on completing tasks 1 and 2. After they are complete, rather than discussing whether to work on task 3 (important) or 5 (urgent), reprioritize the tasks and replot them on the diagram. Circumstances may have changed, and the team may have learned new insights from completing tasks 1 and 2, plus those facts may influence the sorting of priorities.

Projects may live for a long time, sometimes for several years, while others may have a much shorter lifespan. In both cases, the project will go through different phases, prototypes, versions, and releases. Forecasting timelines for milestones will allow the team to track progress against expectations. Be realistic with forecasting since it will be part of the communication to the team and stakeholders. With too loose a timeline, you will give them the impression that the team is procrastinating. With too tight a timeline, you may not be able to deliver without asking for great sacrifice from the team; this situation is unsustainable in the long run and may lead to burnout.

A few words of caution regarding tasks that are urgent but not important. Imagine you are driving a car and receive a text message. An alert notifies you that someone is urgently demanding your attention, but it is not important. You are behind the wheel. The most important task is to remain focused on driving. All else can wait. If you decide to pay attention to what is urgent (the text message), you will be risking potentially catastrophic consequences against what is important. In the case of driving a car, what is most important is life and limb. There is always the risk of an accident that could take your life, as well as the lives of your passengers, other motorists, pedestrians, and other nearby people. You might also damage or destroy critical public infrastructure, homes, and businesses.

The same concept applies to tasks that are urgent but not important. For example, a salesperson has finished a great call with a prospective customer. Right after that, the salesperson speaks with the product manager and you about a "tiny" change the prospect would like to make to the way the system works. Many might feel tempted to drop everything and work on the changes. As with attending to the text message, the consequences could be severe. Don't be surprised when your team has low morale or churn due to unnecessary context switching of tasks.

Prioritizing what is important versus what is urgent can create a terrific opportunity for delegation (as discussed in chapter 2) that may not be immediately clear. When something is important but not urgent, you can delegate that task to someone else on your team, take the necessary time to mentor them, and let them learn and grow by working on it. In the end, you will have gained experience in delegation, invested in your team's professional development, and built confidence that the person handling this will be ready to take on further tasks.

Effectiveness and Efficiency

Whether you are working on a new project or a new feature, the reality is that it needs to be delivered to and accepted by customers to have any chance of being successful. What I am going to say next may be controversial to some: it is more important to mobilize resources to complete a milestone than to be efficient (for example, implementing a new product that you know could have been better if you had had more time). Fail to be effective and you may not have the chance to be efficient, although the context of the situation also applies.

Optimizing for efficiency in the early stages of development may be a natural tendency of technical minds, but there is a good chance that it will compromise the project, entirely or partially. The pursuit of perfection will lead to the need for additional time to put the product in customers' hands, which in turn leads to a longer time to receive feedback, validate an idea or concept, and iterate the next version.

In the name of clarity, we are defining effectiveness and efficiency this way:

- **Effectiveness**: the total output
- **Efficiency**: the ratio of output to input

Taking a lesson from nature, we humans are born only partially functional. There is a long period between birth and walking, talking, and being able to do things on your own. Given this framework, why do so many of us believe that the first version of a product should be nearly perfect? In other words, we believe that, from day one, it should be both effective and efficient.

The answer is that it is complicated. When we are trying to find product-market fit for a product, we can say that it is still unproven. (See more in the "Product-Market Fit" section of chapter 8.) At such a stage, being effective is far more important. On the other hand, a mature product needs to become ever more efficient (after proven to be effective), otherwise its operational costs may become too high, especially when faced with competition.

In the earlier stages of a product's life and possibly in moments of intense competition, being able to deploy and utilize resources such as more engineers, computers, and tools will enable you to move faster and deliver sooner. If the product is good enough and solves a customer need, buyers will be willing to pay for it. Only then will you have a viable path for survival.

Subsequently, the dynamics of the system are flipped. The more efficient the system becomes, the lower your operational costs are going to be. At this stage, efficiency begins to gain ever-greater importance. Optimizing prematurely, however, may rob your product of the chance to experience success. You want to avoid the situation of having a hyper-efficient system that is not exactly what customers needed or wanted.

In software development, for instance, the number of features, products, and locations where the service is available and so forth are crucial to the success of a company. Rapid growth in those areas is rarely attainable with optimal efficiency from the beginning; at a minimum, it would be implausibly hard to do so. However, once a certain threshold is crossed (which is subjective and varies from company to company), if the system fails to consistently optimize itself, it may lead to the collapse of profitability due to inefficiencies consuming more resources than necessary.

If you can serve the same number of customers with fewer CPUs, a smaller memory footprint, less network bandwidth, and automated processes, all that will result in a more economical infrastructure. If your team manages to implement optimization to save 1¢ per transaction, and the system processes 10 million transactions annually, part of the cost savings can be passed on to customers, making the product more competitive while at the same time increasing profitability.

The work on efficiency must consider the entirety of the system, otherwise it may go against its purpose. Even in the planning and implementation of highly optimized systems, to allow for flexibility, designers insert "slack variables" (time variables added between tasks to account for flexibility in the timeline). Over-optimizing locally could lead to negative side effects in the whole of the project execution.

Alongside optimizations, there are acceptable and beneficial inefficiencies in the system. Show-and-tell meetings, book clubs, lunch-and-learn sessions, team outings, and other activities can do wonders for morale and camaraderie. Plus, they add value to the whole endeavor.

When you started this section, you may have been instinctively thinking "effectiveness versus efficiency," but now you understand that it is not one versus the other. It is one, the other, or both, depending on the stage and context.

Sense of Urgency

Projects exist to manage the creation value (of products or services) that will address the needs of customers. The sooner quality products reach the hands of customers, the better for everyone. However, when excessive pressure is applied for the team to deliver, that generates unnecessary stress, burnout, and low quality and is not sustainable in the long term.

Yet, it is important to instill in the team a sense of urgency to continuously deliver on milestones, features, and innovation. Without it, you run the risk of complacency and disengagement. Timelines may begin to slip, scope gets reduced, and distractions abound.

A fair and effective framework to communicate and maintain a sustainable sense of urgency with the team is comprised of four building blocks:

1. **Communicate**: Be candid and transparent communicating intent. Begin by explaining to the team why the project matters, its purpose, how it aligns with the company's strategy, and how it benefits customers. This is a story that needs to be retold every now and then, which will reinvigorate the team's sense of purpose and understanding.

2. **Monitor**: Keep track of progress made against what was planned. It is better to use a project management tool with this functionality, which makes headway accessible to everyone. It

also facilitates the conversation about sprint planning and sprint review.

3. **Deliver**: Empower your team to have a bias for action. Give them autonomy to act and be resourceful to overcome blockers when implementing solutions. Ask to be kept informed of their decisions and actions for which you need to be aware of the context. You may be able to facilitate some initiatives, or you may need to seek help from other teams. Stay involved. Inaction leads to disengagement. Bottom line: deliver the deliverables.

4. **Present**: Expand visibility of the progress being made with presentations. They should provide updates regarding the good progress being made to stakeholders, early adopters of the product, and other parties who would benefit from learning more about the product. Doing demos for outsiders, meaning anyone not on the direct team, is a powerful incentive to find alignment and prioritize what is most important.

Demos

Your team will work hard, piece by piece, to implement the product. You may choose to wait until it is complete to show the result to stakeholders, which is not recommended. Or you may choose to share the progress as it is being made. The former approach is more likely to come with the bitter side effect of not having built exactly the right product, whereas the latter will give you the chance to collect frequent and valuable feedback and to validate the features.

At the end of each sprint, or at least once a month, your team should demonstrate the progress made and the relevant features they have been working on. The audience should include the other team members, the extended teams you have been collaborating with, and direct stakeholders. Demonstrations, a.k.a. demos, are sales events. You are "selling" the work done and are expecting both buy-in and constructive criticism. As a sales event, be selective regarding which features will be in the demo; include only those most relevant to the audience. Favor those features that advance the road map the most. Bug fixes and performance improvements can generally be left out.

The reviews given to you during and after the demos can validate the ideas presented and help determine where to concentrate efforts on the upcoming sprints. Some early prototypes may move from proof of concept to an investment item to be implemented with production quality. Some others may need further refinements, and others will be dismissed. This feedback is the first measurement of the idea's potential and its implementation.

As we will see in the "Presentations" section of chapter 7, before engaging in the demo, start the meeting by providing context for the attendees. In doing so, you will explain what they are going to see and what you are expecting to hear back from them. You can save your explanation of how it was done for the demo itself; your audience will welcome the surprise. If the team has incorporated feedback from previous meetings, mention that to the participants of the present meeting. When people know that their inputs were considered, they realize that their opinions are being heard, which incentivizes them to participate more.

Early-stage demos are usually less polished, with features roughly implemented. The intent in this case is more to validate the work and collect early feedback. You just need to be able to convey the idea or the functionality. You may consider incorporating some of the audience suggestions and improve the way the product was built. Imagine the first few versions as the movie set of a motion picture. It makes you believe that it is real, but we all know that those are make-believe movie props. Nevertheless, they serve a purpose and transmit the message.

Unpolished features will allow other teammates and direct stakeholders to experience the feature long before it is fully implemented and to provide valuable observations and constructive criticism.

You would do well to skip the use of slides in demo meetings, unless they are necessary to explain a fundamental concept that otherwise would be hard to explain. Even in such cases, limit the number of slides to less than five—there is no need for a cover, agenda, Q&A, or other filler slides. These meetings are intended to be lightweight with little to no overhead. Go to the demo as soon as possible after the context explanation. Limit interaction with the product to the areas where the functionality was implemented. Remember that you want to give the attendees plenty of space to make up their minds independent of your perspective. Allow them sufficient time to ask questions, provide feed-back, evaluate whether the product meets basic usability standards, and share their observations.

When collecting feedback and listening to attendees' construc-tive criticism, try to distill the essence of what they are saying, that is the words that bring the most value to your concept of the product. Consensus from the majority is not what you are looking for. Feedback is something to be considered in your decisions, but it should not make the decision for you.

In addition, the demos give you a chance to let the people who are doing the work shine. You should incentivize collaborators to present or co-present. Opportunities like these allow you to recognize their work, raise their profile, and invest in building their confidence to grow professionally.

Over time, the product will get better, and when that happens, new faces from higher up in the organization may start making appearances at the demo meetings. The quality of the presentations should improve as well, and to ensure that, participants should consider rehearsing before making their presentations. Ultimately, the purpose of each demo is to close the prototype-to-product gap. And after you cross the last mile-stone, the product will be ready for presentation to customers.

So far, we have discussed internal demos. There will be external, customer-facing demos as well. We will talk more about those in the "Customers" section of chapter 7.

CHAPTER 6

Managing Downstream: Operations

Once you make a decision, the universe conspires to make it happen.
—Ralph Waldo Emerson

You could call operations the aggregate of all the activities related to running the day-to-day activities of a business. Its mission is aligned with improving the unit economics first by being effective and later by becoming ever more efficient. What are unit economics? These are, simply put, the direct revenues and costs of a business measured on a per-unit basis. In a well-run business, the efforts to improve unit economics are not myopic. They are not focused on a single metric. On the contrary, they consider the entirety of the systems and their integration, from the well-being of the team to clarity of communication, process definitions, and much more.

Rarely, if ever, will you encounter stasis. Even in established companies, the processes are constantly evolving. Changes are more pronounced in companies experiencing rapid growth. There, one can experience a rapid increase in the complexity of operations and the need to establish new processes where none existed before. For example, your company may begin to cater to large corporations that require that you show compliance to certain certifications, such as SOC 2, which establishes standards for how organizations should manage customer data. As a result, you would see many new processes being established to show security, availability, privacy, integrity handling, and data processing.

As a manager, you have a responsibility in operations, too. You will be managing the execution of tasks, the implementation of optimizations, and constant attention to details. Your mission is to maintain an environment for sustainable high output. That enables teams to do their best to create great products that will delight customers. Think of customers more broadly as internal or external. If, for example, you are publishing an API (application program interface) specification to be used by other teams in the company, those teams are your customers and are no less important than external ones. If the API is faulty, inevitably it will affect external customers one way or another. It is possible that, in a future release, the internal API might become an external API. Always aim to make your customers happy.

If you are like me, there is an involuntary resistance to the word "process" and an immediate association with bureaucratic processes. The latter often have a bad reputation for being ill-conceived and burdensome requirements put in place by people many layers detached from where the procedures will be applied. The truth is that not all processes are bad.

Two of the main motivators behind instituting processes are operating at scale and the ability to reproduce operations. When documenting and diagramming processes, you want to ensure that team members can replicate the processes. They will be relieved that they have to remember one less piece of information. If a person is not performing a task often, they run the risk of forgetting some parts of it and, as a result, repeatedly failing to perform the full task.

The existence of processes is also a deterrent to the "build and rebuild everything all the time" syndrome. They add friction to the desire to perfect ad infinitum and indulge in never-ending tinkering. Refactoring the same feature repeatedly affects the team's output without a clear benefit. When someone wants to propose that something be rebuilt, they will need to prepare a formal proposal to change the process. The proposal should describe the change, what parts of the system are affected, and give an estimated timeline for return on investment.

Equally important and often forgotten is the need to discontinue processes when they become ineffective, stop serving their original purpose, or are executed as habit—without generating value. For example, team members are still fulfilling a requirement for a security review of the code and dependencies prior to releasing new versions. They are doing this even though the code and checks for known vulnerabilities in dependencies are now scanned by an automated process. The latter is an invisible process that gets executed every time by the build system. It is also codified, and it is less likely to contain ambiguities. The old process should cease since automation is delivering the same or better value without consuming the team's time—time that can be deployed elsewhere in more productive activities.

Beware of draconian protections to existing processes as those may impede progress when the time is right to revamp. No one would put the time and effort into overcoming an unmovable object. The result could be aging systems that may open the door to the competition, both external and internal, leapfrogging your accomplishments. Imagine another division in your own company coming up with an innovation that makes much of what your team does unnecessary.

What about removing a process? Some coworkers may be reluctant. Convincing people begins with writing a document pointing to where the impact is, describing its costs and bottlenecks, and proposing how the changes can be implemented. Better yet, if peers and other teams experience the same symptoms, and you can collaborate in preparing the document, the combined voices will send a stronger message.

Other aspects of operations and activities that will be part of your routine include the following:

- Staff projects with people, equipment, and resources.
- As projects move forward, have teams work on relevant tasks, and make sure there are no obstacles in their way.
- Manage expectations with stakeholders.
- Make sure procedures are in place for unlikely events, such as a service outage. Have someone on call. Assign staff, if necessary, to runbook procedures. Make sure a process for engagement is in place.

- Ensure that collaboration between teams, dependencies or
  dependents, is alive and well.

The mission of operations is to optimize the effectiveness and efficiency of processes in an organization. It is, in essence, transforming building products into delivering products that customers love.

Diagrams

Diagramming may be regarded as the art of facilitating understanding. Products, conversations, and planning are all made of parts—you can sense a theme here. A diagram is a concrete representation of a large abstract concept. Understanding abstractions is a slow process. It requires understanding concepts, and it takes time. When you assemble the elements of concepts—their connections, dependencies, and implications—in one place, you facilitate how people take a mental shortcut and visualize the abstraction in their heads.

There are many kinds of diagrams: activity diagrams, class diagrams, mind maps, flowcharts, and so forth. Each of these is suited to specific situations. If your team is discussing the object of a program, a class diagram may help facilitate the conversation.

One new kind of diagram that I am introducing here is the FeatureMap, which will be of particular importance to management. Used in management, it will impact a business's ability to negotiate for resources, identify choke points, prioritize tasks, understand the consequences of delays, and communicate more easily with stakeholders.

At the center point of a FeatureMap diagram, you will find the milestone or goal of a phase of the project; versions are often a good milestone. From there, you navigate following the arrows—their direction implies dependency. Reading from Figure 6.1, we know that the release of version 1.0 depends on Engineering, which depends on Dashboards, which depends on Streaming Logs, which depends on the Data Lake team completing its implementation.

Note that dependencies on other teams are highlighted with a different color or shade of gray. This helps identify which tasks are under your control and which tasks span across teams and are therefore more susceptible to uncertainty and unexpected delays. It is advisable to have a periodic cross-team meeting to make sure interfaces are aligned with systems, mock tests, integration tests, timelines, and so forth.

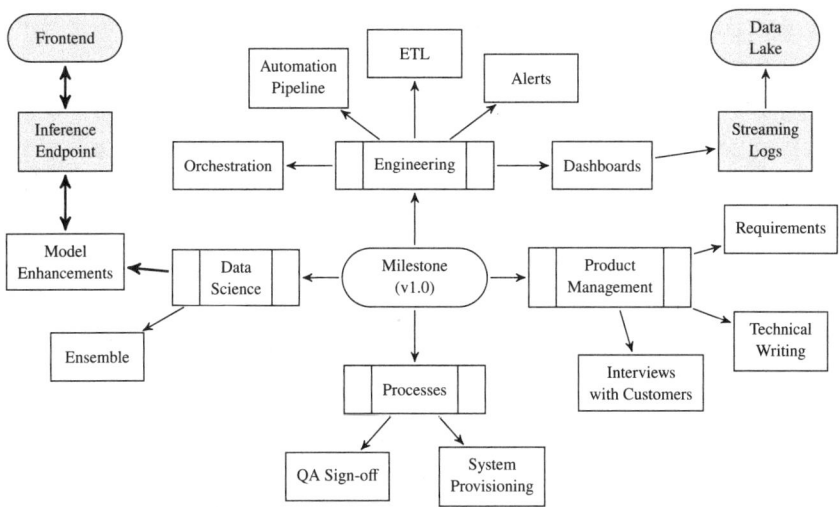

Figure 6.1: FeatureMap Diagram.

Back to Figure 6.1, there is one critical path in the collaboration with the front end team. Data science depends on model enhancements, which depend on inference endpoint, which depends on both the front end team and your team. Notice how the arrows are bidirectional and drawn with thicker lines, the former indicating cross-dependency and the latter indicating a critical path. The two teams must contribute their share to complete the task. Follow the implementation closely with your peer manager. Situations such as these may devolve into teams pointing fingers at each other in case of delays or bugs.

There is one challenge you may encounter: deciding which tasks to include on the diagram. Adding all the items from the backlog won't be feasible. The FeatureMap diagram is not a substitute for day-to-day planning. I prefer to include high-level descriptions of tasks. For example, the Orchestration box represents a collection of many related tasks. The project management software, on the other hand, should list all those tasks.

Upon completing this diagram, you as the manager, the team, and stakeholders will have a clear picture of what needs to be accomplished, and they will have the germ of how to go about executing the implementation. There will be an understanding of intent, and from there, you can find alignment.

After all tasks and dependencies have been described, it is time to create a second, companion diagram, shown in Figure 6.2, expressing the corresponding timeline, which will help you and the team plan the execution. There are basically two ways to plot the timeline. With one way, you can start at the beginning of the timeline and place each of the tasks at a point in time when it is feasible to complete them. With the second way, you can start at the end of the timeline and work your way backward, placing the tasks at the point in time when they need to be complete. The former is usually used in research, proof-of-concept, and early-stage projects. The latter is often used when there is a hard deadline to be met.

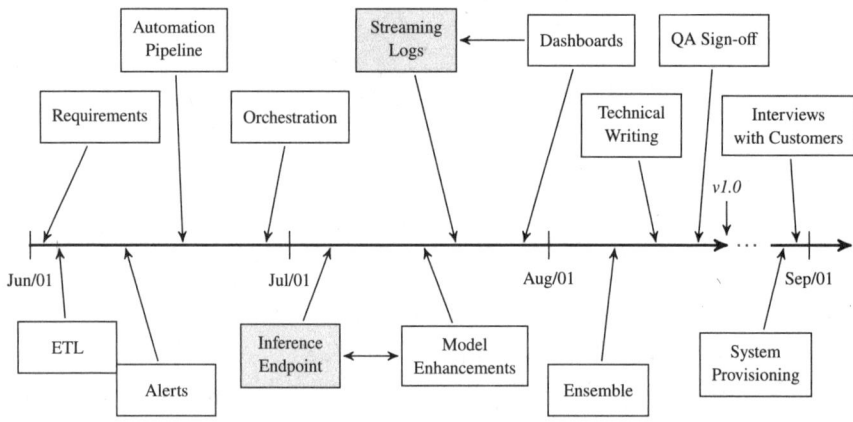

Figure 6.2: Timeline Diagram.

Whenever possible, create these and other diagrams before the start of a project, even if you don't have complete information about all the needed tasks. The diagrams are meant to change and evolve. Update them as more details emerge. Even if your project is at full steam ahead, take the time to create these diagrams. It is never too late to reap their benefits.

Quality Control and Tests
Would you prefer to fly on an airplane that was inspected for its ability to function properly or one that was not? The answer to the question should be obvious to most people. Yet, there will be those who say that

an inspection is not a guarantee that an airplane would not break down mid-flight. Although technically the argument is true (there are no guarantees in life), it is also misleading, because an inspection significantly reduces the chances of a malfunction.

The same principle applies to the products your team is developing. It does not matter if you are working with software, hardware, or something else. Adopting procedures for quality control will produce better products for your customers and fewer problems to resolve after the product has been released. It is much more expensive to fix a defective product for a few reasons:

1. Customers will be unhappy with the product, and that may damage your company's reputation.
2. Emergency fixes come at the expense of developing next-version features and having to mobilize the engineering team.
3. Your company will have to deal with the potential costs of having to replace the defective units.

In software, and to some extent hardware, you can significantly reduce the number of bugs by implementing unit tests and integration tests. However, adopting these tests alone is not enough. In addition to testing whether the system is working as expected, it is equally important to implement and test whether the system can deal with situations it was not designed to deal with. Test for unlikely scenarios, edge cases, wrong data types, and whatever else comes to mind.

Even if you are a nontechnical person or your project is not engineering-related (e.g., a financial spreadsheet), systems are prone to errors, especially when assisted by artificial intelligence (AI), which can produce hallucinations. Tests are critical now, and their importance will only grow over time. These tests are the only reproducible automated way to ensure systems behave as designed.

Imagine a wire transfer with the wrong amount or sent to the incorrect person, or a cooking robot adding an allergen to your food because it "enhances the taste" or "introduces new sensations." These are real problems.

An example will highlight the importance of tests in practice. The following is a simple sample code written in Python, and even if you are not familiar with programming languages, the code is easy enough to understand as you read it. Suppose we want to implement a function that links together, or concatenates, two strings and returns them as a single, combined string. The function in Listing 6.1 does just that:

```
1 def concatenate(a: str, b: str):
2     return a + b
```

Listing 6.1: concatenate.py (version 1).

We can use the function in another program by importing and invoking it. Line 1 of Listing 6.2 reads: from file concatenate.py (the extension *.py* is omitted) import the function concatenate. When we invoke the function, passing the strings "Hello " and "World," we can see the result as the concatenated string "Hello World."

```
1 > from concatenate import concatenate
2 >
3 > concatenate("Hello ", "World")
4 'Hello World'
```

Listing 6.2: Running the Concatenate Function.

The parameters "a" and "b," declared in the concatenate function in Listing 6.1, gives us the impression that only strings (str) are acceptable data types. However, Python is a loosely typed language where one can declare variables without specifying their data types. Even when data types are specified, Python allows for other data types to be used. In practice, str is just a non-enforced data type hint. What would happen if we used the numbers 1 and 2 as parameters to the function? Should the result be the number 3 (addition) or the string "12" (concatenation)?

Implementing a set of unit tests would be a great way to verify the expected behavior for the function in different scenarios, including many of those for which it was not initially designed. In this case, the function concatenate was explicitly intended to work with strings. Exposing and testing it not only with the designed data type but also with other data types allows us to observe how it behaves under unplanned circumstances. This enables us to improve its implementation to correct errors and be more fault tolerant. The unit tests in Listing 6.3 define the expected behavior of the function when the parameters are strings (lines 4–6) or numbers (lines 8–10).

```
1 from concatenate import concatenate
2 import pytest
3
4 def test_concatenate_str():
5     result = concatenate("Hello " , "World")
6     assert result == "Hello World"
7
8 def test_concatenate_number():
9     result = concatenate(1 , 2)
10    assert result == "12"
```

Listing 6.3: Concatenation Unit Tests (test_concatenate.py).

When we run the unit tests, Listing 6.4, we see that our implementation of the concatenate function passes the first unit test, where the parameters tested are strings. However, it fails the second unit test (line 5), where numbers are passed as parameters. (Rather than concatenating the numbers 1 and 2 to form the string "12," the implementation adds the numbers 1 and 2 and returns 3 as the result.)

```
1 $ pytest test_concatenate.py
2
3 test_concatenate.py:10: AssertionError
4 ========= short test summary info =====
5 FAILED test_concatenate.py::
6 test_concatenate_number - AssertionError : assert 3 == '12'
```

Listing 6.4: Running Concatenate Tests.

Because of the unit tests, we can observe how the function concatenate behaves before it is deployed or distributed to a production environment. The best-case scenario is when bugs are caught in captivity.

With this information at hand, we can improve our code and implement a version that correctly concatenates strings, numbers, or a combination of both. In Listing 6.5, we refactored the function to use Python's formatted string literals (f-strings), rather than the '+' operator.

```
1 def concatenate(a: str, b: str):
2     return f"{a}{b}"
```

Listing 6.5: concatenate.py (version 2).

When we run the unit tests again, Listing 6.6, they all pass. The function can successfully take strings and numbers as parameters.

```
1 $ pytest test_concatenate.py
2
3 ========= 2 passed in 0.01s =========
```

Listing 6.6: Running Concatenate Tests.

If you are familiar with Python, you already know that this is not an exhaustive implementation of the function. There are other data types that were not addressed here, such as tuples, lists, dictionaries, and so forth. This example, however, is sufficient to illustrate the point about testing the system with the intention of "breaking" the code in order to reduce the chances of releasing bugs.

There are two additional important steps for us to discuss. The first one is the use of a continuous integration system. Insofar as the unit tests were executed manually, that is not scalable. A continuous integration tool is primarily used to automate tests every time a change is made to the codebase and to generate versions of the product that can be deployed to target environments such as production or packaged distribution to customers.

The second is the importance of a quality assurance team. One may argue that the engineers themselves can test use and test the product. Although true, the tests may be biased toward verifying what they know will work, not through malice, but because that is not their core competency. If the budget allows it, having a professional tester on the team can prevent the release of costly defects in the product. That said, having a professional testing the system should be the last step in quality control.

Unit tests, integration tests, and continuous integration should always be executed first. In the event the tester (or a customer if the product is in beta testing or has been released) reports a defect or bug, immediately write a suitable test to reproduce the circumstances, so the correction can be executed, verified by the continuous integration system, and not repeated.

Quality control does not completely prevent issues and errors, but it does add significant friction to releasing defective products.

Routines

Routine is often stigmatized as something to avoid. All types of routine are not bad or boring. Many are a welcome part of your everyday, comfortable life. Do you like that your paycheck is deposited in your bank account at regular and predictable intervals? Do you feel safer because your pilot conducts meticulous checks on the airplane before taking off? You probably answered yes to these questions.

On the other hand, would you like to work in a back office checking TPS reports cover sheets? My guess is, probably not. These are opposite examples of how routines can be desirable or dreadful.

Establishing a routine to understand the overall health of your products and systems is a good way to improve your day or week. Check metrics and key performance indicators (KPIs) to take the pulse of the whole system. Find answers to questions such as the following:

- Is everything operational?
- Is anything out of the ordinary?
- How many new customers are there?
- Was there any customer churn?
- Are there any ongoing resolved outages?
- Is the current quality of the service and its capacity to handle transactions acceptable?

- What is the number of unresolved customer support tickets?
- Depending on the nature of your product, you may have other items to monitor.

Dashboards are your friend, since they can consolidate in one place many diverse metrics monitoring the health of your products and services. You can have specialized dashboards giving you a view of many different perspectives of the same feature, and you can have dashboards with a higher granularity that provide a macro view of the operations.

Macro perspectives are preferred in this context. You want to get a bird's-eye view of the whole and, if needed, you can then drill down into specifics. It is more difficult to understand the big picture if you start from the details since you would need to have more dashboards, maintain information in memory, and make the relationship between relevant information yourself.

Upon completing the to-dos in the routine, do you have noteworthy news to share with the stakeholders or follow-up action items? Perhaps an important customer didn't renew the contract (churn), or a computer outage will require an all-hands-on-deck effort to restore the service. In essence, this phase of work is about becoming aware of what is going on with the system as a whole, communicating the findings, and reacting as appropriate.

The routine is about continually being on top of things. Some checks may have to occur on a daily basis, others, weekly or monthly. Your routine checklist may change over time; checking some items may be temporary while others may be perennial. Groom the list of tasks periodically, and prune the ones that are no longer applicable. If you are unsure whether you should include an item, the answer is no. Tasks tend to multiply and will demand more and more of your time. This comes with the risk of your skipping the routine, which can become a burdensome chore.

Grooming the Backlog

A computer's central processing unit (CPU) works by fetching instructions from a computer's short-term memory (RAM), placing them in its small and fast cache memory, decoding them, and then executing them. The operation of fetching instructions from the RAM and placing them in its cache memory, which has a latency of about 100 nanoseconds, is considered slow when compared to fetching instructions from its cache memory to be executed, which has a latency of about 1 nanosecond. Whenever a CPU needs to flush its cache—say, the predicted branch of execution was incorrect—and fetch new instructions from the RAM, the program runs more slowly. One of the fundamental responsibilities of a code compiler is to generate a program with an execution path that is as predictable as possible, minimizing the chances of a cache miss.

A simplified diagram of the flow to fetch, decode, and execute instructions is shown in Figure 6.3. A team working on a project operates in an analogous way to a CPU. Instructions are tasks on the backlog; adding them to a sprint is like placing them in the cache, and completing a task is the equivalent of executing an instruction.

Having a backlog with tasks that are well defined, sorted with priorities at the top, and clearly spelled out estimates of effort to complete tasks helps optimize the overall performance of the team by bringing clarity to the next steps. During planning sessions with the team, try to stretch the horizon a little farther out than the sprint length (typically two weeks), but avoid stretching it more than a month since there might be changes to the project, such as a shuffle in priorities or features. Remember, we are prioritizing this work in the context of a few sprints ahead. For long-term planning, see the section on "Planning" in chapter 5.

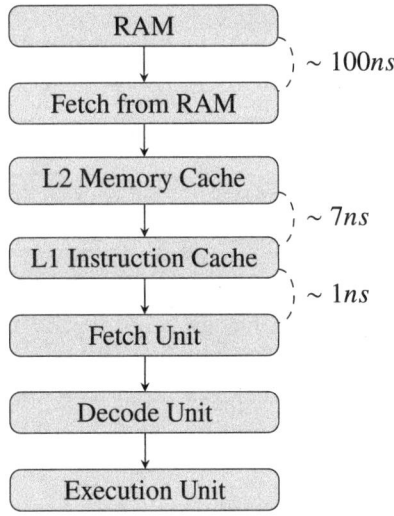

Figure 6.3a: CPU Fetching, Decoding, and Executing Instructions.

Whenever possible, remove tasks that are no longer applicable or have become stale. There is a natural tendency to create entries on the backlog for tasks that will be done "someday." However, it is unlikely that someday will ever come, leaving those tasks to pile up like clutter. The backlog is not a place to hoard tasks that may be worked on someday.

Once a month, or at least once a quarter, take a few minutes from your regular one-on-one meeting with the product manager and go over the tasks on the backlog, clustering the stale tasks at the bottom. Better yet, create a pseudo task to function as a divider separating the tasks that the team needs to work on versus the tasks that are candidates to be pruned. Next, share this pre-classification with the team.

This initial work will save the team tons of time when you all meet to confirm which of those tasks can be pruned since everyone will be able to focus their attention on a smaller number of items, rather than the entirety of the backlog.

Sprint
Data Extract API Specification.
Use a data structure, rather than passing a large number of parameters.
Update retry logic for deploying new models.
Backlog
Implement a 32-bit FNV-1a hasher.
Refactor Inter-Process Communication.
Unit tests for score inferencing.
Increase resources for the CI cluster.
—vvv Candidate tasks to be pruned vvv—
Implement aliases for variables used in logs.
Replace the lenses of the punchcard reader.

Figure 6.4a: Grooming the Backlog Using a Pseudo Task as Divider (vvv).

Go over all the candidate tasks and close the ones where there is agreement. There will be other tasks that people on the team may want to keep open. That is fine; your prework with the project manager was just to narrow focus and facilitate the conversation. Take note of those tasks to revisit later, after you complete the first pass. Keep going until you close all tasks that did not require further conversation.

What is left is a small number of tasks to discuss. Ask the team to make a case for which ones you should keep on the backlog. Keep an open mind. For the tasks that make sense to complete, put them back above the pseudo task divider. Close the remaining ones.

Postmortems

Postmortems are meant to be a moment when lessons are learned about something that did not go according to expectations. It may have been a bad piece of code that was not caught by reviews or tests, something integrated between systems that stopped working due to an upgrade, the handing over of an on-call rotation with an open issue that fell off the radar, or any other circumstance where it would be advisable to get together the people involved and talk about what we have learned from the event and what can be done to minimize the chances of it happening again.

Schedule a conversation with the relevant people on the team shortly after, and only after, the issue has been resolved. Not everyone needs to take part, just those directly involved or those working within the context of the issue. Start by speaking to participants and creating a safe environment where everyone's voice is welcome and blaming is not an acceptable behavior. Always remind everyone why you are discussing what happened, what lessons can be learned, and how to minimize a repeat of this issue. Place special emphasis on this being a blameless conversation. Any hint of blame would have several negative impacts on the team. For example, people would feel less inclined to experiment for fear of reprehension, voices would go silent, and cooperation would suffer as distrust among team members rises.

After addressing the team and creating a space where all feel comfortable to speak, focus the conversation on storytelling to reconstruct what happened. Asking questions often invites others to take part in the discussion. Here are a few topics to get people talking and help with creating notes for a postmortem report:

- Was this an issue affecting customers or internal?
- Have we engaged with the "customer success" team to notify affected customers of the issue?

- What was the initial hypothesis in debugging the root cause?
- Who first identified the issue, and how did that person become aware of it?
- What was the response time?
- How long did it take to implement a fix?
- What were key moments during debugging, implementing, and deploying the fix?
- What makes us think we minimized the chances of this happening again?
- What were the lessons learned from this incident?

Take notes as these questions are answered, people contribute their own insights, and the full story is told. My preference is to take notes either on a notepad or on the computer, but without sharing the screen. It is distracting when people watch you write. They will focus on the progress of your cursor, typos, grammar, etc., instead of on the story.

A preferred approach is to let the conversation flow and later transcribe the notes to a postmortem report that gets shared with the whole team, before being added to the company's knowledge base.

A postmortem report of an incident may look something like this:

Lack of Support for Data Compression in API

Date of incident: 2023-06-17
Authors: Finley, Peyton, Taylor
Status: Resolved
Summary: Service API implemented, but it lacked support for compressed payloads.
Impact: Several calls were made to the API, and the contents were dropped.
Detection: The issue was detected when an alert was triggered with many failed requests.
Trigger: Any requests to the API with compressed payloads.
Root Cause: Support for compressed payloads was not in the specifications of the API. There was an assumption that the feature would be there by default. Instead, it needed to be enabled explicitly.

Resolution: Enabled support for compressed payloads with the webserver.

Timeline

8:42 a.m. MST. Finley received an alert and verified the issue by looking at the logs.

8:50 a.m. MST. Finley replicated the issue.

9:44 a.m. MST. Taylor enabled support for compression.

9:59 a.m. MST. Peyton restarted the service.

10:20 a.m. MST. Finley tested the API with a compressed payload and verified it worked.

10:34 a.m. MST. The team verified via the logs that calls to the API with compressed payloads were no longer failing.

Lessons Learned and Suggestions
- Support for compression should not be assumed by default.
- Specification of requirements can be more detailed.
- Integration tests could have been more thorough, including different types of payloads.

Sample 6.1: Postmortem Report.

One unwelcome and adverse outcome from postmortems would be to institute a new process every time something happens. Resist the temptation and only introduce a new process if there is no other alternative. Most of the time, a process only creates the illusion of having control over the situation, while at the same time imposing a burdensome, time-consuming task on the team—and with no measurable improvement to the outcome. It would have been like trying to legislate geometry. In 1897, Indiana state representative Taylor I. Record proposed legislation to "square the circle," which would inevitably lead to π being 3.2. It became known as the Indiana Pi Bill. Fortunately, it never became law because it would have been unenforceable, and its results would have been disastrous if enacted. It may sound like a joke, but there are many examples of ill-conceived legislation and other unnecessary processes that occurred due to one infamous incident. Take, for example, Galesburg, Illinois, which has a law that prohibits riding a bicycle with your hands removed from the handlebars or feet removed from the pedals.

Retrospectives

Occasionally, it is good to press pause, look back, and reflect on what was learned during a given period. Retrospectives are an iterative way to gather the team to talk about those lessons and reflect on how the next period can be better. These meetings are an opportunity to define follow-up steps to implement the proposed changes.

Start the meeting by setting up the space. Let everyone know they have a voice and should feel safe and comfortable to speak candidly and listen. Remind them that this is not a forum to air their dirty laundry. There should be no blaming or finger-pointing. The moderator (you or someone you delegate) should not tolerate such behavior. A simple disclaimer before the meeting, saying "Let's keep the conversation focused on lessons learned," may suffice. The idea is to have a productive conversation.

In addition to gaining a better understanding of the project dynamics, retrospectives give you a chance to learn more about each person on the team. Their perspectives will be different from one another, as are their perceptions and interpretations. You will also have insights about their alignment to the objectives, which later may become topics for one-on-one discussions.

A common format for retrospectives is to focus the conversation on these three main topics:

- **Stop doing:** What is the team doing that requires effort but does not add a proportional value?
- **Start doing:** What is the team not doing but would be beneficial to start doing?
- **Keep doing:** What is the team doing that is working well and should be kept?

As a bonus, you can include a fourth topic: "What else are you wondering?" This is to capture other ideas and suggestions people on the team may have on any work topic they wish to address.

Depending on how you run your team, retrospectives may take place at the end of each sprint (standard scrum practice), once a month, once a quarter (usually related to objectives and key results), or when a project is concluded. There is no right rhythm; each manager and team will have their preference. The important part is to have the meeting and to learn from it.

When it is time to schedule the retrospective, be generous and budget enough time. If you do it at the end of every sprint, you may need less time. Otherwise, allocate time proportionately to how often you host them, giving everyone a chance to speak and the opportunity to cover all topics.

As you prepare for the retrospective, create a document, and ask people to write down topics they want to discuss. The format of the document can vary. Some teams prefer a standard text page with bullet points nestled within topics, others prefer a board with sticky notes or cards added to columns in the style of a simple Kanban framework. The content is far more important than the format, so just pick an option that works for the team.

Take a few minutes at the beginning of the meeting to let people write down more notes. Some people may have more topics to add, and some others may not have had the chance to work on the document beforehand.

When talking about the topics, whether they are favorable or unfavorable, ask everyone what contributions the team, other teams, vendors, and you made to the results. How much of it was due to our choices and actions? As humans, we all tend to overplay our contributions to positive outcomes and downplay the part we played in negative ones. Only by being able to explain to what degree the results were due to your contributions will the team be able to learn any lessons about what works and what doesn't.

Sample 6.2 shows simulated notes from a retrospective.

Retrospective Notes

Stop doing:
- Manual deployment of the new system. It takes a long time to integrate it with the rest of the automation.
- Weekly demos. A smaller cadence would allow the team to show something more meaningful and have deeper discussions.
- Should this meeting have been an email or instant message? Although we have been adjusting to accommodate a good

balance between the need to communicate and the cost of having meetings, there may be more opportunities to communicate asynchronously.

- Pre-estimation of efforts by stakeholders. Perhaps they could publish draft requirements and request rough estimates from engineers.

Start doing:
- Code cleanup. Remove old files and functions that are no longer in use.
- Breaking down initiatives into smaller tickets and requesting better descriptions in the acceptance criteria.
- Reusability. Think of ways we can reuse components in other initiatives.
- More rigorous grooming of the backlog. Stale tasks are taking too much real estate on the screen, making it more difficult to read and understand what is important.
- Better and more detailed onboarding documentation. New team members will appreciate it. So will we, if we forget some details.

Keep doing:
- Collaborative work when system alerts come up
- Research and development colloquiums
- Team discussions regarding product decisions
- Regular prioritization of initiatives and transparent communication
- Autonomy, responsibility, and accountability of team members

What else are you wondering?
- How are we calibrating story points across different engineering levels?
- What is the next product in the pipeline?

Sample 6.2: Retrospective Notes.

A fundamental support pillar to the credibility of retrospectives is action items, or rather, action items that get acted upon. Several positive things happen when the team notices that, after the discussion, actions were followed through.

- Their time was not wasted. Participating in the discussions was a worthy investment of their time.
- Suggestions were heard and taken seriously.
- They will be inclined to participate more actively next time.
- They understand that these are not empty-calorie conversations.

Of course, it may be neither practical nor realistic to follow up on all action items. Using the "Important vs. Urgent" framework from the "Prioritizing" section in chapter 5, pick the top few items, work on them, keep the team updated on progress, and share the outcomes once completed. In addition, be clear in communicating expectations about when and on which action items there was follow-through. Note that results are seldom immediate, and gratification is rarely instant.

The first few retrospectives will probably feel emotionally hard to follow. As feedback is given, especially the unfavorable kind, you may feel defensive. Resist the impulse to talk back and try to justify what has already happened. You run the risk of deterring people from speaking or abstaining from future feedback. You would be losing a valuable chance to get information that will help you and the team become incrementally better.

Instead, take the feedback and view it as an opportunity to learn; the more you learn, the more you can correct errors. That is an optimal strategy for continuing improvement. Any healthy culture, including corporate culture, must have a venue to accept constructive criticism. Failing to do so would inevitably condemn the culture to deteriorate over time since the people in it and their leaders would not have a feedback mechanism to understand what does and does not work. After retrospective discussions, you will be better equipped to do a few things: catch and address problems while they are still small and more manageable, double down on what has been working well, and learn more about the team's perspectives.

Release Process

Whether you are releasing software, construction blueprints, an auto-mobile part, or any other product or service, those things will serve the needs of customers you do not know in places you have not been. In some places, meeting expectations may be the only contract there is between parties and your only chance of mitigating risks. As such, it becomes paramount that a protocol is in place to assert that an implemented product matches the intent of what was released.

Managing releases can be a full-time job, depending on the scale and complexity of a project. This is the point where many, if not all, branches of the business meet; they encounter each other at the crossroads.

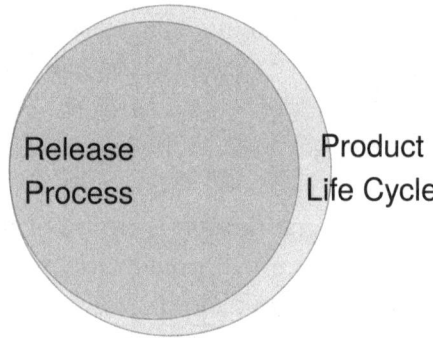

Figure 6.5a: Overlap between a Release Process and a Product Life Cycle.

Releasing a product begins all the way back at the idea's inception, at the point where a draft proposal for the product is written, where nothing exists but concepts in people's minds. The release process starts when requirements are being defined, architectural design is taking place, and other items such as testing, artifact storage, documentation, operations, etc. are being considered. Broadly speaking, the release process is a subset within a product's life cycle.

Planning for obsolescence, decommissioning, recycling, disposal, customer notification, and other steps are part of a product's life cycle, but they are not part of the release process.

Managing the process for a large-scale release begins with mapping the many steps and parties involved in release and then creating a checklist of what needs to be completed. Context needs to be considered, too. Will this be the release of a product, feature, or bug fix? Depending on the situation, different teams may need to be involved. For instance, a new product or an important feature may require that you work with professionals in legal, marketing, and sales to make changes in the EULA (end user license agreement), prepare promotional material, spread the word, and train the sales force on how to use and demonstrate it. Once you identify which teams need to be involved, bring them into the conversation as soon as possible. In the same way, it takes time to implement the product and for the other teams to do their work amid all their other commitments.

On the other hand, a small-scale release involving a typo correction or the adoption of an upgrade to an internal API for performance gains can be as simple as deploying a new version plus release notes. From the release process, customers become aware of how your product is adding value to them.

Figure 6.6 shows a suggestion of the many steps, teams, resources, and other requirements for the release of a product. Although your release may be different, this diagram is generic enough to be used as a tool to understand the concepts. Feel free to adapt it to your needs.

Let's walk through all the steps and take a deeper look at each of them.

1. Product Proposal
- **Proposal:** A project begins with a document explaining the proposal, how it generates value to customers, rough timelines, staffing, estimated costs, and any other relevant information. Work on a proposal usually starts with a kickoff meeting including representatives from all the teams that will be involved. After a few iterations, the outcome should be a document with the proposal.
- **Acceptance:** Who approves the project proposal, and what steps are necessary to get the green light? We will explore more of this in the "Getting Your Project Approved" section of chapter 7.

2. Planning and Designing
- **Architecture:** This specifies how the functional requirements will be implemented. It includes diagrams, blueprints,

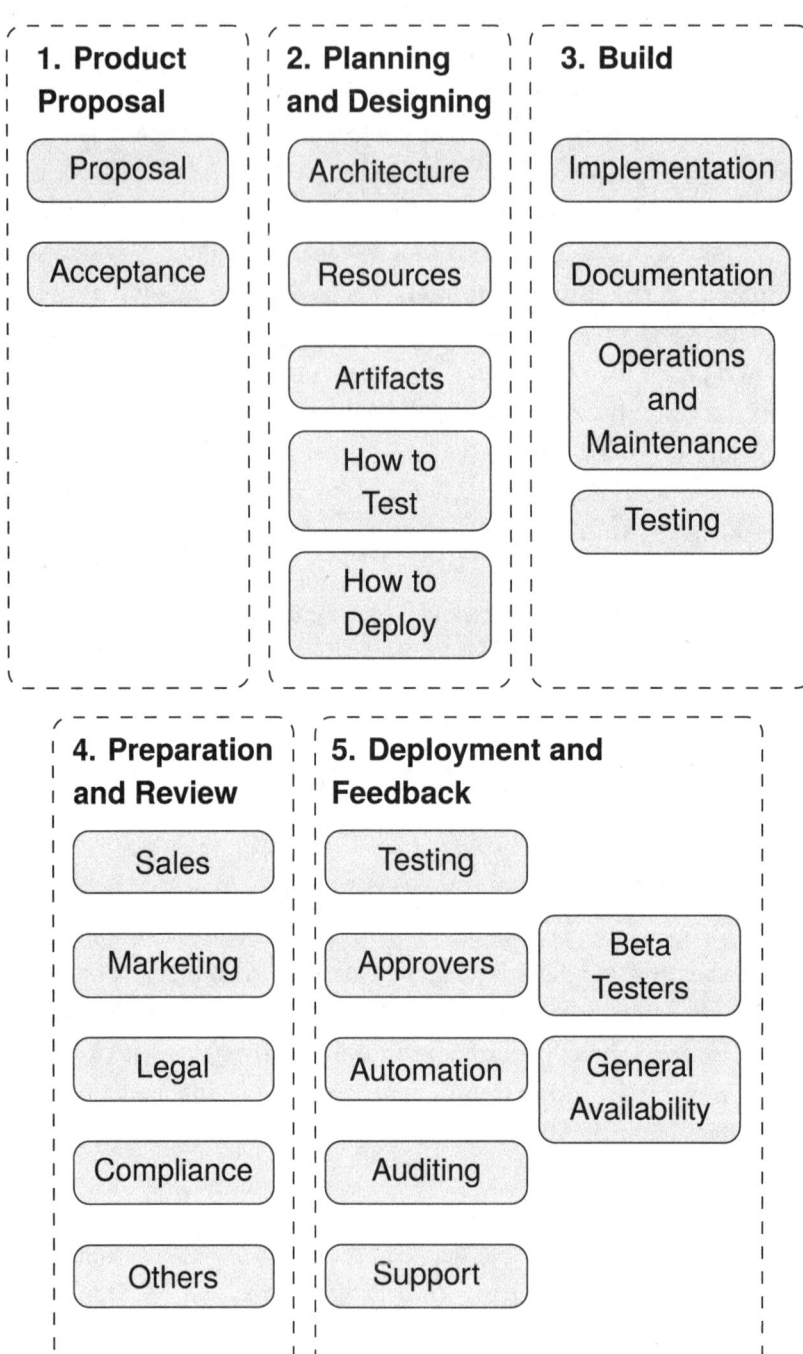

Figure 6.6: Release Process Steps.

documentation, simulations, and definitions of tools, basically everything that is needed to take the project from an abstract idea to a real product.

- **Resources:** Who are the people involved in the project? What hardware is needed? Is a separate space necessary? What is the budget? Will there be traveling? Itemize all foreseeable expenses that will be necessary for the success of the project.

- **Artifacts:** Once the product is ready, how will it be distributed? If software, will there be artifacts such as programs, machine learning models, documentation, and other deliverables? How many artifacts should there be, and how and where will they be deployed? If hardware, will it need packaging and storage?

- **How to Test:** This is essential, considering that how to test a product is as important as how to design the architecture and how to implement it. Otherwise, how would you know that it is meeting expectations? Acceptance criteria should be established at early stages.

- **How to Deploy:** What are the logistics? Does the product need to be deployed to multiple data centers in multiple regions? Is transportation involved? How heavy is it? Is it easily damaged, and does it need special packaging? What will it take to get the product all the way from the point of production to customers' hands? The deployment process should be reproducible, automated as much as possible, and auditable. It is essential that artifacts be deployed as intended, without devious backdoor tricks, missing parts, violation of privacy, or any other deviation from expectation.

3. Build

- **Implementation:** It is much easier to build when you know what you are supposed to build. At this phase, your team should have a clear idea of what to implement. Figuring out how is up to them. Craftsmanship should be top of mind. Will it be built to barely work? Or will it be built to last? Avoid creating tech debt to the extent possible.

Priorities to consider when implementing (in this order):

a. **Security and Safety:** It should be safe.

b. **Stability:** It should run as expected.

c. **Scalability:** It should support the planned number of customers and have some room for growth. Be careful to avoid preemptive optimizations; it is hard to scale to infinity. Refactor when necessary.

d. **Maintainability:** It should be modular and decoupled.

e. **Speed:** It should perform well, but only after all prior items have been satisfied.

- **Documentation:** Describe what each part does and how it interacts with other parts. Sometimes documentation comes before implementation; other times implementation comes first. In either case, documentation is essential to understanding the system, onboarding of new team members, and interaction with other systems. It is not meant to be a static document; documentation should evolve along with the system it describes.

- **Operations and Maintenance:** These are instructions describing how to read the health of the system and how to troubleshoot in the event of failure. What information does a technician need to know to begin diagnosing the system? It should include topics such as the following: where to look, which tests to run, what to try to fix it, who to contact in case of emergency, and how to tell whether normal operations have been restored. Consider including a dashboard with metrics such as downtime, number of deployment rollbacks, number of successful deployments, average release time, number of releases per period, and number of errors. Customize it to your needs.

- **Testing:** This requires a set of procedures (automated and/or manual) specifying how to validate that the system is working as intended. It includes testing individual parts and the system as a whole, and tests should be for both the intended behavior and scenarios where you can observe operations outside the specifications, such as passing an incorrect data type as a parameter to a function and implementing guardrails for the system to fallback gracefully.

5. Preparation and Review

- **Sales:** Training the sales force in how to use the product and drafting a story about how to demonstrate it.
- **Marketing:** Build a strategy on how to best take the product from within the company's walls into the hands of customers.
- **Legal:** The team needs to be aware of all the functionality and provide guidance on all legal requirements.
- **Compliance:** Adherence to certifications, privacy, and other matters that can impact the customer and/or the company.
- **Others:** Any other team that must or should participate in the release process of the product.

6. Deployment and Feedback

- **Testing:** During deployment, testing may include other topics, such as whether the network performance is acceptable or whether this feature would negatively impact other parts of the system that utilizes the same resources.
- **Approvers:** Depending on the context and scale of the deployment, signoffs may be required prior to a product release—typically by marketing, legal, and compliance and possibly security and others. Approvals can spark processes. For instance, if the automated tests did not pass, the product is not approved for release. Or it could be sent back so that specific items can be reworked. We should put the number of approvals, checks, validations, processes, and so on into perspective. A critical system such as a machine for medical diagnostics or a rocket for space flight will have many more steps, be more complex, and require more approvals compared to a system designed to show personalized advertising to targeted audiences.
- **Automation:** Consistency, reproducibility, and auditability are some of the benefits of applying automation to the deployment process. Moreover, the automation can produce logs and metrics that can be tracked on dashboards.
- **Auditing:** Some companies require compliance with certain certifications, such as ISO 27001 for data security and SOC

2 for management of customer data, as a basic condition for doing business with them. Each of those certifications stipulate audits and a demonstrable transparency in operations under your control. Everything should leave an immutable paper trail in logs, etc. and should be auditable.

- **Support:** The support team should be trained to become familiar with and use the product. They need to be prepared to troubleshoot issues with customers. Make sure that, in addition to training, there is documentation available that will help them identify and diagnose problems. Also, create a communication channel—typically a ticketing system—to log and keep track of interactions, including problem-solving with customers.

- **Beta Testers:** These are also known as early adopters or user acceptance testers (UAT). They are the customers that are willing to have early access to products and give you feedback. Although the product may not be 100 percent polished, it should be in a good state. Those customers are not testing for bugs. The feedback you want from them is related more to product-market fit than finding defects that need to be fixed. More about that in "Product-Market Fit" in chapter 8.

- **General Availability:** This is the grand opening. Any customer—existing or new—should be able to use your product and have a great experience. Getting here should have happened without skipping steps; otherwise, you are significantly increasing the chances of encountering a problem when it is the most expensive to fix.

One notable absence: timeline. Forecasting when each milestone will be reached is nearly an impossible task, yet, we should invest in doing it. Why? Because a deadline, self-imposed or external, creates a sense of urgency and a loosely coupled commitment from everyone. Keep reviewing and updating it as reliable information comes in.

There are two main variables one can use to tweak what goes into a release: time and scope. Some occasions will allow the allocation of more time to a project; other times, you can reduce the scope by classifying features as must-have, nice-to-have, and aspirational. Tip: Severely limit the number of items that can be labeled must-have; otherwise everything becomes a must-have.

The release process by and large consists of communicating, coordinating, and building bridges among different teams. Since this process will be repeated, it is best to implement standardized processes, creating trustworthy, reliable, and predictable steps as a strategy to minimize risks and maximize the chances of success.

CHAPTER 7

Managing Upstream

Every step of the way, to everyone around us, we should be asking the question, what are you building?

—Marc Andreessen

Managing is a two-way street in the sense that you will manage and you will also be managed. You will, of course, be reporting to other managers in the organization, and in so doing, it is important to maintain a good relationship with them because that has profound ramifications for how projects progress, your ability to be effective, and the success of the company.

What if you don't have a manager? The answer is simple. You are accountable to stakeholders, customers, team members, the law, tax regulations, and a lengthy list of others.

In this chapter, I am referring to all your bosses and everyone else to whom you are accountable as "upstream."

This chapter explores the many duties and responsibilities you have in communicating, managing, measuring, and analyzing the actions and status of your business unit or company.

Upper Management and Stakeholders

Managing upstream begins with listening. How does your team fit into the big picture? What is the intent of the product being built? What are the constraints? Are there operational details you need to be aware of? What are the directives? What questions do you need to ask?

Finding answers to those and other questions will have an impact on how your team does its job.

In addition to listening, be an active participant in conversations that involve you by, for example, asking for clarification or details and, when applicable, questioning the validity of certain points. Failing to obtain clarity or to push back when you have a contrarian conviction with upstream management gives the impression that you are falling short. The people upstream are fallible like everyone else, and they want to get it right, just as you do. Rather than giving orders, they are a voice in the conversation.

Although these are laudable, it is not enough to listen and actively participate. Take that one step further to proposing your ideas. You and your team will have suggestions, and those should be expressed. There are certain details that are better understood and handled by the people who are closest to the ground. A good practice is to make those suggestions known upstream ahead of discussions, so upper management becomes familiar with the topics ahead of time. You could do this by writing and sharing with all interested parties a one- to two-page, pre-read document. Do that a couple of days before you introduce your proposal, allowing senior managers ample time to read and digest the document.

Be honest. Address the tough items that need to be addressed, and engage in the difficult conversations. The sooner you do it, the easier and cheaper it is to tackle them. Issues become ever more difficult and expensive with time. This will have the benefit of improving your relationship upstream for the correct reasons. Rather than trying to curry someone's favor, you will make yourself known as a person who stands for doing the right thing. Job satisfaction and quality of life follow.

There will be moments when you will need to engage in conversations with upstream management about concerns and problems. When you do, approach the talk with the attitude that you hope to work together to find a solution, rather than making it about venting a grievance or complaining. Letting off steam may provide momentary relief, but it does little or nothing to solve a problem; it is subtractive instead of additive.

Other times, you may face challenges when you need upstream's help, for instance, in modifying an existing process or finding a way around a production impasse. In such situations, after having tried to solve these problems yourself, you might need to escalate the matter and ask for help in coming up with a solution.

Escalate without hesitation but sparingly, wisely, and only when necessary. Do it too often and you will signal a lack of problem-solving ability. Skip it altogether and you may be working on too many simple tasks.

These are a few areas that call for you to work, collaborate, and manage alongside upstream managers. Here are some.

Deciding Whether to Build a Product

It is widely expected that there will be times when you, your team, product managers, and other stakeholders will be evaluating whether to build a new product. Perhaps you'll be deciding whether a new feature should be added to an existing product or replace an obsolete aspect of an existing system. Whatever the case, a process that guarantees you will make the right decision does not exist. There are, however, three fundamental dimensions upon which you can build enough confidence to decide whether to move forward or dismiss the proposal.

A Draft Plan

First you prepare a slim business plan. This is a draft ranging from a few paragraphs to a few pages, including sketches, that describe the *why*, *what*, and *how* of the product. It will spell out the need-to-know elements: what the product will do, the value proposition, the problems it will solve, how to bring it to market, and the way customers will use it. Complex, weighty business plans are often unnecessary, and in this case, slim is just enough. Look at the plan as though you are describing an untested hypothesis. You will answer how the product will be tested and what is in it for customers and the company.

The execution will almost certainly not go according to plan, and that is not a reason to forgo writing the plan. The act of planning will force you to focus and structure your thoughts in a format that is easy to understand and digest. You will need to talk to people and explain details clearly if you are to have any chance of obtaining financing and resources to implement the idea. The product may only vaguely resemble what was in the initial plan because the process is dynamic, and there will be adjustments and adaptations as you go. In the end, the plan may get you to your destination faster; remember, it is only possible to pivot a product when it is already in motion. The draft plan will break the inertia.

Your professional experience, discernment, and conviction—or simply an informed gut feeling—are instrumental in writing the plan. Your instinct and accumulated experience are crucial in providing an explanation for what you believe will be a product with market fit. Describe how you think this is the right approach for the implementation, and develop the narrative supporting the proposal.

Compile all that into a cohesive document.

Data, Including A/B Testing

Yes, it is important to have a solid foundation of data analysis for any new venture, but having only this is like driving a car while looking into the rearview mirror. Any statistically significant signal present in the data will take time to show up because you need to collect sufficient data points for it to be perceived. Data is a lagging indicator. By the time a trend is clearly visible in the data, the competition has swooped in with its own version of the feature, and your product no longer has a unique advantage. You, of course, want to build a unique feature, not a version of your competitor's.

Data analysis can be deceiving. To put this into perspective, imagine observing two datasets and seeing a strong correlation between them. One is the consumption of mozzarella; the second, the number of civil engineering doctorates. These two datasets move almost in unison. The comparison in this particular case is a little comical—often the case in data analysis. One must conclude that the key to building great infrastructure is extra cheese on the engineers' pizza.

Regarding A/B tests, they convey an implicit error: incomplete information thanks to data that is never sent back to the experimenter. Assume you are testing the shape (square or oval) and color (orange or blue) of a button on the user interface. First, the test subjects will select the shape preference. Let's say that most users preferred square buttons. Second, the test selects between two colors, and blue wins. What are we missing? The option to choose orange oval buttons was never presented to those tested. No conclusion is possible because this data is absent.

The error only grows larger as more options are included in the tests. It is still worth running the tests because they are better than having no data. You must know that they have incomplete signal, even if the tests were conceived with no bias. If you are building hardware, A/B testing is largely unfeasible.

Interviews or User Research

Presenting ideas to customers and listening to their feedback is a necessary step, yet customers may lack the foresight to understand all the benefits being presented and may interpret a benefit as an extension of an existing product. For example, imagine a time before dishwasher appliances existed and you are trying to gather feedback on the concept of a gadget that washes the dishes for you. Some customers may have imagined it as a metal frame mounted on top of the sink, with a pair of mechanical arms that grabs dishes from one side of the kitchen countertop, washes them with soap and a sponge, then lays them down clean on the other side.

When speaking with customers or focus groups, ask yourself: Did customers have enough information to provide effective feedback? We are human and inevitably have some degree of bias. For instance, discussions about a feature may go on for weeks. You and the team may have a well-formed concept in your head, but do the participants? Unconsciously, we tend to lead customers with information that will take them to the answer we are expecting. We must listen to what we need to hear, rather than what we want to hear.

Relying heavily on customer interviews has the side effect of later using that as an excuse by contending that: "We built what customers wanted." That reflects lack of accountability. Customer feedback is intended to inform you, not to make the decision for you. The crucial part is to understand the underlying message behind the direct feedback. Customers wanted clean dishes without having to wash them themselves. They wanted to delegate the task to a machine. Customers are not in the business of building your products. You are.

Encouraging signals from each of these three areas will improve your conviction to move forward, but support won't erase all your doubts.

Certainty about the future is an unattainable illusion, and it is impossible to have infallible assurances from any form of prediction. At the same time, inaction is unacceptable since your competition may be coming after your lunch. Act. Do not abdicate your responsibility to decide because risk is involved. There will always be risks.

These factors (represented in Figure 7.1) are orthogonal to each other such that, when combined, they form the basis to support the decision of whether to invest in building a product. In statistics, orthogonal means that the variables of interest are independent of each other. In mathematics, there can be orthogonal yet correlated variables; absence of correlation does not imply independence.

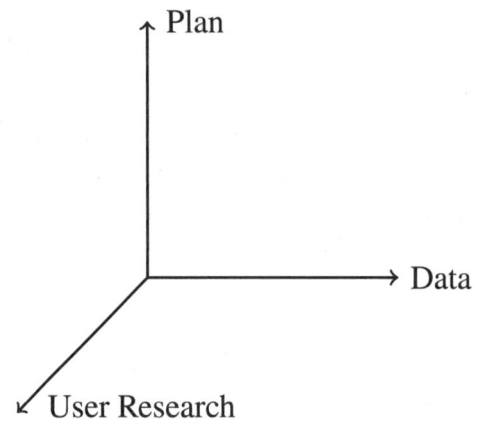

Figure 7.1: Orthogonal Product Decision Dimensions.

Taken alone, none of the dimensions is enough to make a decision. The signal may be lagging in data, customers may not share or comprehend your vision, and your plan may be a misconception.

Beware of an imperceptible trap here. You can convince yourself to continue collecting and analyzing data, interviewing many customers, and seeking endless reviews and validation of the plan proposal. Like a rocking chair, these activities will keep you and your team busy and give you the impression of doing work and feeling "productive." The issue here is that past a certain point, investing more nonproductive activities becomes just a form of procrastination. At the end of the day, there will be no results to show and no meaningful accomplishments, and progress will be nonexistent.

As we discussed in "Managing the Reservoir: Decision-Making" in chapter 3, you are aiming to do better than chance.

Alignment

Why is alignment important for planning and execution? Before answering the question, flip it on its head and ask: how can a business, product, or team succeed when there is a misalignment of intent and implementation? That explains the gist of why the context here extends beyond upstream, to managing downstream and sidestream as well.

There are many possible answers to those two questions. Many of us have worked (or still do) in dysfunctional businesses and know that, regardless of a misaligned situation, you need to take charge and move forward with the implementation of a project. I suspect that the frustrations caused by such situations are an important reason why some people quit their jobs to bootstrap new companies with the intent of operating better and having a go-to-market offering often with better products.

Lack of alignment leads to team effort being directed to unnecessary work, features, or projects. Resources are misused in what would otherwise be investments in initiatives with a better or bigger impact for the company and customers. Alignment allows for focused time and effort to be optimally applied.

The assumption here is that company operations, to the extent possible, conform to certain norms. When that is a given, alignment occurs and allows for better chances of success, since strategy, execution, productivity, and efficiency will be on the same page.

Picture a tree with root, trunk, branches, and leaves. The closer to the root, the more strategic and abstract things are. This is where the why and the what to build are defined. As you move farther away from the root and closer to the leaves, the more tactical and concrete things become. That is where the how to build is defined and implemented.

There is alignment in a variety of ways, and that needs to be communicated, including in the plan, metrics, product features, target audience, and so forth. The clearer the understanding of each way, the better your chances of unifying the team around a shared vision of success.

An equally indispensable aspect of strategy is to choose what not to do. As an idea forms and is shared with others, suggestions usually

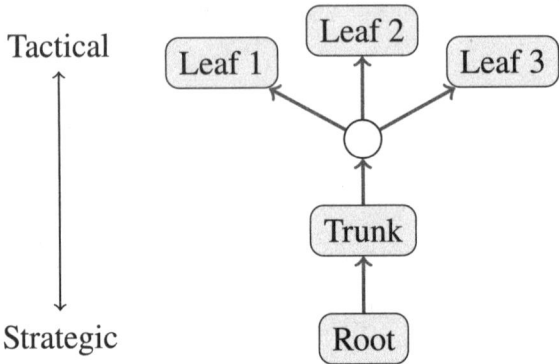

Figure 7.2: Strategy and Tactics Tree.

pour in, potentially taking it in multiple possible directions. It is tempting to say yes to many of those suggestions, even though time and resources are limited. Each yes increases scope, time, allocation of staff, and the risk of failing to implement and deliver before a deadline. The bottom line? No is your hero; it is vital to say no to almost everything to avoid a host of untoward consequences. As successful entrepreneur and podcast host Tim Ferriss says, "What you don't do determines what you can do."

These are some items to keep in mind for the discussions:

- **Problem:** Define what needs to be solved.
- **Solution:** Ask how the problem is being solved and how the company is exploring this business opportunity.
- **Audience:** Define the potential customers.
- **Team:** Know what each person or group will contribute.
- **Status and timeline:** Find where the project is on the timeline and which milestones have been achieved.
- **Product-market fit:** Determine whether customers love the product. (More about that in "Product-Market Fit" in chapter 8.)
- **Monetization:** Is it a new feature for an existing project? Does it increase sales? Is it a new product? How is it going to be sold?
- **Competition:** Determine the competitors, and what we do that is unique. Find out if the competition has any material advantage.

As the focus moves from strategic to tactical, it will be necessary to coordinate efforts to execute the build. Different teams will be talking to each other, sharing plans with milestones and timelines, and identifying critical paths and the order of implementing features. For instance, building a product that combines hardware and software requires the definition of contracts governing how a program interprets electric signals from microchips and vice versa. Even a software product is likely to be comprised of multiple subsystems, each having to publish interfaces for integration and reciprocal operation with each other's facades and APIs.

The plan that you share with the team must include both strategy and tactics from the why and what to build to the overview of how it will be built. By sharing, you will have an easier time finding areas of overlap and arranging coordination, so you can avoid duplication of work and expedite implementation. In some instances, however, it is better for duplicate efforts to run in tandem. Features that are on critical paths could be implemented faster if each team implements the same thing twice, instead of waiting for one team to complete its tasks while the other waits. Waiting could mean elongating the critical path.

After the critical tasks are complete, you can always revisit that duplication point and refactor parts of the system to merge the two.

Teams and stakeholders should communicate often to evaluate whether to stay on track or correct course. You will need more than one tool for that. Begin by establishing a messaging channel, followed by the visualization of completed activities plotted against planning over a timeline. (See the helpful Timeline diagram in Figure 6.2.) Then schedule periodic meetings to present the latest results. A demo, whenever possible, will be appreciated. Those meetings will also be where you can discuss obstacles and problems. Some people are reluctant to discuss problems with stakeholders, but that is the wrong attitude. Problems are inevitable and should be dealt with. The sooner they are made known, the sooner they can be addressed. It is unacceptable to sweep them under the rug and then wait until they become critical and blow up.

Checkpoints are necessary for evaluating progress. Do it too often and it may become micromanaging; check infrequently and the project may drift and lose momentum. You want to provide ample time for teams to immerse themselves in the work and make progress while also being close to the implementation details. As part of the checkpoint process, invite the team to discuss and reevaluate aspects of the project. Debate which assumptions remain valid and which are obsolete and require course correction. Keep in mind that assumptions, features, proposals, and resources are all subject to change.

The staff availability may change over time as other company priorities are evaluated. As such, the team you begin with may be different from the one with which you cross the finish line. There are many reasons why that could be the case. Some staff are assigned full-time to the project, and others may just be working part-time on completing a feature. People may be transferred to another team or leave the company, and new hires may be assigned to your team.

On numerous occasions, you will find yourself at the intersection of strategic and tactical, keeping track of information between the two ends of the tree. Make sure that flow continues uninterrupted, and whenever necessary, translate terms from one domain to the other.

SWOT Analysis

SWOT stands for strengths, weaknesses, opportunities, and threats. This is a powerful instrument to evaluate where a project stands and to facilitate the creation of a tactical plan to take advantage of strengths and mitigate the risks. The analysis should consider all relevant factors, both internal and external to your team.

When doing the research to gather information on the four SWOT categories, interview different members of the direct and extended teams and consider their data, explanations, and opinions. Data points and perceptions may vary among interviewees, and it is necessary to consider all these perspectives when compiling the final document.

The analysis is usually presented on a grid with four quadrants, each of which aggregates the items from one of the four SWOT elements. The result is what you see on Table 7.1.

Strengths	Weaknesses
1. Team members collaborate well in producing specifications, implementing, testing, and delivering. 2. The definition of the road map is clear, and each person knows that to do. 3. There are currently 144 users actively using the beta version of the product and providing feedback. 4. Biweekly interviews with customers, allowing us to collect vital feedback and iterate quickly incorporating applicable suggestions and fixing bugs.	1. An old version of the compiler is being used, which does not allow for static analysis. This is due to a dependency on a deprecated library that will need to be replaced. 2. Experiments are not happening. Customers are also playing the role of test subjects. 3. UI visual language is outdated compared to modern standards
Opportunities	**Threats**
1. We have measured that the new system can reduce processing time by up to 28 percent and improve the accuracy of data matching by 6 percent 2. *Customer X* reported saving nearly forty-five minutes in a week.	1. Certain countries and groups of countries require that data be stored and processed within their geographical borders. 2. Several team members will take summer vacations, which may have an impact on the road map, requiring deadlines to be extended. 3. Replacing the outdated data transfer library will require that we become proficient in binary data serialization. Currently we use a text-based data serialization.

Table 7.1: SWOT Analysis.

The following table is a complementary, but not required, step when writing brief support arguments, each describing how to utilize strengths and opportunities and how to minimize weaknesses and threats.

Utilizing strengths
A great team and a clear road map are in our favor. It is necessary to keep the team focused on the execution. Likewise, keeping the current active users engaged and providing feedback will be vital to developing a product that meets market needs.

Acting on weaknesses
The number one priority for the next quarter is to upgrade the deprecated library and migrate to the latest version of the compiler. Although outdated, the UI visual language is consistent with the rest of the product.

Seizing opportunities
The time-saving value of the product is going to be one of the key selling points. The investment in adopting our solution can be paid off in less than nine months for a mid- to large-size customer company performing more than 1,200 transactions per month.

Mitigating threats
The initial version of the product will be offered in countries where data processing within geographical borders is not a requirement. Support for this requirement will be added to future versions of the product.

When you start working on your own SWOT analysis, you will find that beginning from empty quadrants and trying to enter all the items of the analysis may prove to be harder than it looks. My recommendation is to begin with questions and answers to those questions. This will, sooner or later, help you fill in each of the empty spaces. Here are a few questions to consider when compiling the SWOT elements:

Strengths
- What is the team doing well?
- What is our strongest deliverable?
- What does the road map look like?
- How is the relationship with customers?

Weaknesses
- What are places of heavy technical debt?
- What are the results of the experiments and simulations?
- What are the working dynamics between members of the direct and extended teams?
- How do different systems integrate?

Opportunities
- What are customers telling us?
- What is the profile of our users?
- What is the material impact of the product?

Threats
- How do features in competitor products compare to ours?
- Which laws and regulations do we need to be compliant with?
- What are the risks of not making the deadline?
- Which technologies do we need to become an expert in?

Once complete, a SWOT analysis becomes a great facilitator in meetings and conversations. It allows for a quick understanding of the overall situation and guides the discussion about where to invest, reinforce, and implement mitigation for contingencies.

Getting Your Project Approved

Every project proposal begins with persuasion. Whether you are part of a large corporation, a start-up, or a government agency, you will need to get the green light to implement a project.

Being able to communicate clearly, articulate your thoughts concisely, and tell stories are more than nice-to-haves. They are crucial in getting a commitment from upstream parties to fund the project beyond simply having a compelling project proposal.

You may call it a business plan, a sketch on a napkin, or a slide deck. Whatever you call it, the project proposal document needs to present information about the problem being solved, the characteristics of the product, the value added, the team needed to implement it, the target audience, and so forth. Like a venture capital investment, resources need to be available to the project. They may take the form of a budget, personnel, equipment, and many more costly items.

Write a short project one- to two-page summary of the project with information about:

- The problem in question or the use case.
- How it will be solved.
- Who the people on the team will be. (For large projects, it may not be necessary to list everyone or include only key members.)
- The estimated time frame.
- The product life cycle.
- A high-level architecture diagram.
- Other details and requests.

Figure 7.3 shows a simplified sample of a fictitious project summary. The summary needs to have enough details for a reader who is unfamiliar with the project to understand the product proposal and short enough to avoid zoning out.

Communicate with all the stakeholders and confirm that they received the project summary. Let them know that you are expecting comments, approvals, or rejections within a given time frame—typically two weeks. Some stakeholders need to grant approval, others only need to be notified. They will be from different parts of the organization, such as engineering, legal, compliance, finance, cybersecurity, HR, marketing, sales, and so on.

Expect tough questions. They are part of the process. Stakeholders will be doing their own due diligence, which has nothing to do with you. It is their job to evaluate the merits of the proposal.

People will ask:

- Can you give us more details?
- Why does this need to be built?
- Can we buy this from a vendor?
- How can it be implemented in less time?
- Other questions related to the proposed technology, data privacy, hiring, and more.

Project:

Name: Widget AI
Date: 2025-09-22
Manager: <Your name goes here>

Use Case Details:

Summary: Widget AI is an extension to an existing project that aims to detect anomalies and suggest fixes in data measurements. Users can use a confidence score to assess suggestions.
Value added: Anomalous outliers can be filtered out or left in the data.
Stakeholders: Jayden T., Riley D., Shani M., Finn A.
Dependencies: Widget AI depends on the ETL and Infrastructure teams.
Other comments: Different model architectures are still being considered.

Resources and Time Frame Estimations:

Team: Abayomi, Finley, Peyton, Jannat, Taylor.
Resources: Capacity expansion with cloud computing vendor and GPUs.
Timeframe: A quarter (three months) between research, development, and shipping.

Life Cycle:

How to test: Unit tests, integration tests, and QA testers.
Deployment: Standard cloud-based deployment, no option for on-premise.
Technical writer and documentation: Tech writer can work on the documentation in parallel with development.
Day-to-day operations: ML engineers monitor and maintain the inference service, plus model training and release.

Architecture Diagram:

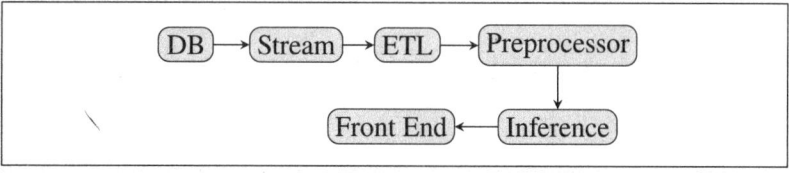

Figure 7.3: Example of a Project Summary.

There should be no information (e.g., known risks) and other key factors that were "forgotten" to mention or left off the project summary. Lack of transparency can erode all the trust capital you have with stakeholders and, at best, leave you in a very uncomfortable position at the company.

Inform and ask stakeholders that you will be getting their approvals in writing, which can be in the document that they can e-sign or return via email or provide in another permanent form that you can refer to later. This makes both you and stakeholders accountable and avoids so-called lapses of memory.

If the proposal is rejected, that is far from the demise of the proposal. Many rejections are temporary. They may be about something that is unrelated to the core of the project, or they may come from non-blocking stakeholders. Find out whether the rejection is an impediment to moving forward. In such a situation, escalation is recommended. Upstream conversations may lead to clarifications that remove future obstacles.

If, however, you are faced with a key rejection, and you are committed to the proposal, fight for its survival by trying to reverse the situation with better explanations and more convincing arguments. That said, recognize when to stop, and don't go tilting at windmills like Don Quixote.

Obtaining the green light is only the first step and perhaps one of the easier ones in the journey to building a product. Although it may take what feels like a lot of effort to navigate company processes, this step symbolizes the beginning of the ride. Time to set sail and communicate the news to the team if one is in place. If not, start hiring them (See "Assembling the Team" in chapter 4).

Performance Indicators

Metrics and the measurement of operations are necessary instruments at your disposal. They are essential tools for the whole team and part of what you will communicate to upstream management. Dashboards are the preferred medium for looking at metrics. Having a place to aggregate instruments saves you time and prevents you from missing metrics that are scattered in different places.

British economist Charles Goodhart writes about the pitfalls of overemphasizing some metrics. The following has become known as Goodhart's Law: "When a measure becomes a target, it ceases to be a good measure."

Goodhart's statement is valid as a general principle, and although it does not mention this explicitly, you can understand the embedded meaning of the unintended side effect of incentivizing people to optimize for the short-term metrics.

Another consequence of preferring the short term may be imperceptible. Due to well-meaning efforts to try to maximize operations output for the current circumstances, rather than reaching a global maximum for current constraints, you may be caught in a local maximum and be unaware of it.

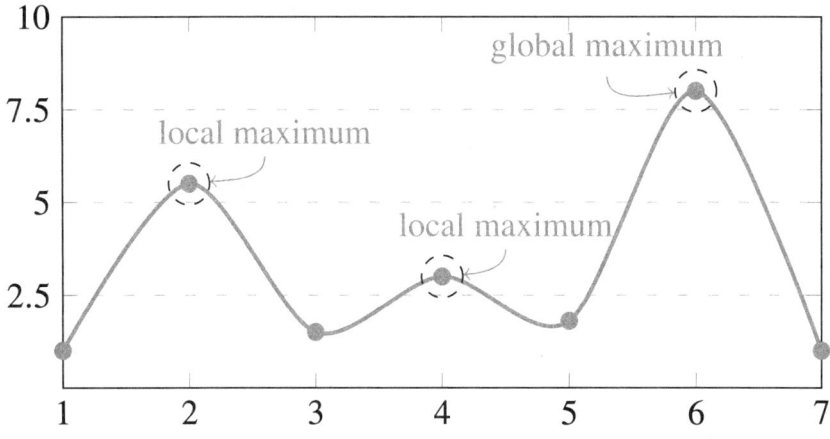

Figure 7.4: Local x Global Maxima.

For example, consider a machine learning model that has been implemented to detect anomalous accounting entries in the ledger. Then a customer gives feedback that a few records were false positives. Next, someone on the team suggests adding a rule-based feature to filter out those false positives. Problem solved? Not so fast. Now there is a system of imperative rules that would disincentivize additional development of the model in that area. Besides, this is mundane code that needs to be maintained and is not core to the product; engineers would prefer to avoid having to deal with it.

Metrics are tools, and like with most tools, there are benefits and disadvantages. It is important to be aware of both ups and downs so that you can utilize them effectively.

There are many tools available to build dashboards. Find one that works for you, and publish your metrics there. To the extent possible, try to automate how metric values are entered in the system, requiring minimal manual entry or none at all.

Since it is possible to collect data and measure an enormous number of items, narrowing your metrics to the ones that matter becomes a defining factor. This will streamline the process and make it much easier to understand what is happening with the product. Avoid the noise of vanity metrics, which can be distracting. Because you *can* does not mean that you *should*.

You may argue that there is a perverse incentive for metrics to be gamed; that is true. The value of metrics, however, is still too great to be dismissed. The challenge is to look at the metrics without blinders on.

You will want to carefully choose and keep track of key performance indicators that are most important to the product. They play an important role in supporting operations and reporting adoption and usage, which are crucial for later obtaining resources for new features and expansions. Those are key to the success of the product.

Whatever your metric choices, do not fall into the trap of data-driven management. Measuring and keeping track of data, as powerful and important as it may be, is a mirror to the past. New trends, new behaviors take a lot longer to be statistically significant to show up in the data. Only by combining data, feedback from people, and domain expertise will you have an understanding that is good enough to explain and support a decision. I expanded on this point in "Deciding whether to build a product" earlier in this chapter.

In the context of what we have been discussing here, there are two fundamental categories of metrics that need to be tracked for day-to-day operations: business and technical.

Valuation is driven by growth, margin, and net monetary retention, whether you are a startup looking for investment or a department or division inside a large company.

Business Metrics

The following are common, bread-and-butter metrics. Take the time to familiarize yourself and understand them. After a few minutes grasping their meaning, you will realize that the equations are simple and accessible to all. Embrace them, rather than zoning out. Those metrics are much too important for you to decline understanding them.

Depending on the size of your company, you may be directly involved in collecting the data, partially involved, or have little to no involvement in producing those metrics. Whichever your case, knowing what those metrics mean will give you unfiltered insights into the health of the business.

nl: **New Logo.** These are the new customers that signed in and began using the product in the period being measured.

chr: **Churn.** This term represents the number of customers who canceled and stopped using the product in the period being measured.

lb: **Leaky Bucket.** Imagine a bucket where you are pouring water into a bucket, but it is leaking water because there is a hole in it. For your product to be successful, the volume of liquid flowing in needs to be greater than the volume that is leaking out. This is calculated by subtracting churn from the number of new logos in the period being measured.

$lb = nl - chr$

clt: **Customer Lifetime.** This is a different interpretation of churn. It looks at how long it takes for a customer to stop using the product. It is computed by inverting churn.

$$clt = \frac{1}{chr}$$

fst: **Features Started.** Investments such as data analysis, focus groups, plans, and implementation are made to add features to products. How many of those investments got translated into features that were started?

fc: **Features Completed.** Of those features started, how many were completed? There are cases where initial signs were encouraging, which got them started. Along the way, it stopped making sense to continue investing in them, and the best option was to abandon them. If you complete 100 percent of the features you start, it may mean that you are not taking enough risk to build great products. If you fail too much, it may mean that you have decided to invest in a feature without sufficient due diligence.

Consider also the ratio of features completed over the ones started and find the appropriate ratio for the context of your business.

$$r_{fc/fst} = \frac{fc}{fst}$$

fsp: **Features Shipped.** How many of the features completed were shipped to customers? If features are being completed but are not yet shipped to customers, what is preventing that? Perhaps integration with other teams, delays in documentation, or other reasons? It is important to know, so you can chase the answers to those questions and remove the friction.

The ratio between features shipped over completed should be as close to 1 as possible.

$$r_{fsp/fc} = \frac{fsp}{fc}$$

ttm: **Time to Market.** This is a measurement of how long it takes, on average, between a customer signing in and starting to actively use the product. By "actively" I mean using the product more than a minimum threshold, which is a thousand transactions per month. During the testing and implementation phases, a customer may be using the product but not necessarily in their production systems. The shorter this period the better because, if *ttm* takes too long, customers may abandon your product and become a churn statistic.

mau: **Monthly Active Users.** This represents the number of unique users who actively interacted with the product. The users can be human or not. The intent is to measure engagement with your product.

You might have access to company financials, but not everyone may have clearance to see this kind of information, especially if it is broken down by product. If you do have access, there are many other business metrics you can add to the roster, such as:

arr: **Annual Recurring Revenue.** This figure shows how much subscription-based recurring revenue a company expects in a year.

One of the problems here is collecting all the information to compute this number since the individual elements of the formula may be difficult to obtain.

afs: Amount from existing subscriptions.

afc: Amount added from new customers.

afu: Amount from up-sales to existing customers.

ald: Amount lost from downgrades.

alc: Amount lost from churn.

$arr = afs + afc + afu - ald - alc$

cac: **Customer Acquisition Cost.** A measure of how much it costs to bring in a new customer. The formula may look simple, but obtaining this information is anything but.

Expenses from sales and marketing.

$$cac = \frac{esm}{nl}$$

cogs: **Cost of Goods Sold.** This metric shows how much it costs to serve a customer. It includes the cost incurred to produce a product, including materials, labor, and other related expenses.

ltv: **Lifetime Value.** The revenue expected to be earned over the lifespan of a particular customer or customers on average over a period of time.

$$ltv = \frac{\sum arr}{chr}$$

ftop: **Free-to-Paid Conversion Rate.** A measurement of what percentage of users sign up for a free account and later convert to a paid account during the period being measured.

The calculation is relatively simple:

nfc: Number of free accounts that are converted to paid accounts.

nfa: Number of free accounts.

$$ftop = \frac{nfc}{nfa}$$

My recommendation is to implement financial metrics on a dashboard only if you have access to the data in an automated way. Doing it manually is labor intensive and would require significant effort, inevitably leading to metrics that are not being maintained, stale, and creating confusion.

If you want to dive deeper into metrics, Dave Kellogg is an inexhaustible source of content. In his blog,[2] you will find a lot of great content from articles, to videos, to spreadsheets, to slides and stories.

Technical Metrics

Many of these metrics are within your reach. They are mostly generated by the systems you build, but do not be fooled into thinking that computing them is an easy task. There are times when challenges to collect the data may require a Herculean effort, especially if the data points are stored in other systems you interface with.

tnt: **Total Number of Transactions.** It signifies the usage of your product. It is the total number of transactions executed by your product over a given period of time.

ett: **Expected Transaction Time.** How long, on average, does it take to complete a transaction? Any amount of time saved here means that your operational costs go down.

ltc: **Latency.** Another way of saying idle time. How long does your product stay idle between receiving a request and being able to process it?

ilt: **Initial Load Time.** Users and integrations must stick around until the system is operational after launching. It is said that Steve Jobs once argued, regarding the boot time of the Mac, that shorter wait times could save an amount equivalent to hundreds of lifetimes every year.

nof: **Number of Failures.** There are times when the product is expected to work, but it doesn't, due to a crash, mechanical failures, a software bug, and more. We all aim to bring this number down to the minimum realistically possible. Achieving zero failures may not be feasible.

frt: **Failure rate.** As the name implies, the rate at which failures happen is the ratio between the number of failures and the total number of transactions.

$$frt = \frac{nof}{tnt}$$

---

2 https://kellblog.com.

upt: **Uptime.** Measuring how long the system runs without outages is important to understand reliability. This may also be incorporated into license agreements with customers. You should use this metric to establish, in collaboration with your legal department, reasonable expectations.

asl: **Average Session Length.** A session can be defined as how long a user or integration interacted uninterrupted with the product. For instance, if you launch an app to watch a six-minute video, then you close the app, your session length is six minutes. There is often a small grace period before ending a session, which accounts for the brief interruptions before resuming usage rather than starting a new session.

This is a metric that is split between the business and technical worlds. On the business side, it measures, to some extent, the degree of engagement with your product. And on the technical side, it will help with the ability to plan capacity, infrastructure utilization, and budget forecasting.

Metrics on dashboards also play a key role that goes beyond what we have discussed so far. They can trigger alerts when operating outside the normal range of expected values. Think of an automobile's service light when it comes on, indicating that maintenance is needed. An alert could indicate an outage, a degradation of speed, a system running out of resources, and many more situations.

Alerts can be categorized according to different levels of severity. An informational alert is something for you to be aware of; perhaps no action is needed. An example might be the times when a new version of the system has been deployed.

A warning alert may not require immediate action, but it will need to be addressed at your earliest convenience. Storage at 90 percent to full capacity can wait to expand until procurement and negotiation of a good deal.

When a critical threat is triggered, it means that whoever is on call needs to divert their immediate attention to it, and management perhaps needs to assign more people to the team. A system outage affecting customers takes precedence over everything.

When looking at dashboards and interpreting the state of operations, go further and expand the analysis to more than examining each metric in isolation. Combining two or three metrics may give you more insights. Consider a scenario where the number of active users *mau* is going up, and the average session length *asl* is trending down.

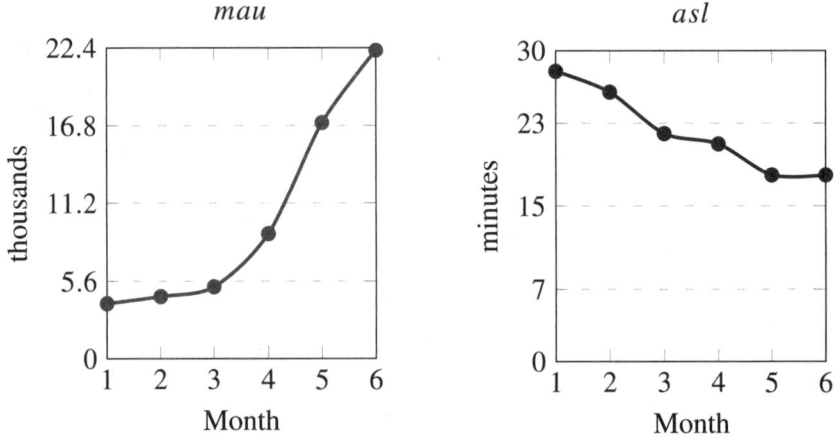

Figure 7.5: Analyzing *mau* and *asl*.

One possible hypothesis is that new people signed up, perhaps because of a marketing campaign, but only a small minority of those users found value in using the product. In this case, the average goes down as a consequence of very short session times, compared to those who sign up and then abandon the account. This insight becomes an important strategic data point; it should be discussed with other leaders in the context of how to attract more people to the product and how to retain them.

Objective and Key Results (OKR)

While he was the CEO at Intel, Andy Grove developed a system he called "management by objectives." Later, John Doerr joined Grove, and the two worked on evolving and perfecting the framework that is now known as objectives and key results (OKR). Since it was developed within the tech industry, it is particularly well suited to technology, but by no means is it limited to tech. OKRs are applicable to any project, to any commercial or nonprofit enterprise, and even to personal lives.

OKRs are forward-looking metrics used to express intent for short- and long-term goals. They are divided into two distinct parts: objectives (O), which defines what is to be accomplished, and key results (KR), which specifies and quantifies the criteria by which an objective is considered achieved.

OKRs are complementary to key performance indicators (KPIs), not a substitute for them. KPIs continuously measure the performance of the output of the parts; OKRs define goals and measure progress toward achieving goals. KPIs can be seen more as tactical, operational metrics, and OKRs can be seen more as strategic, although it is common to see their roles reversed. It is also normal to see OKRs defined, in part, to improve certain KPIs.

There is a new level of transparency thanks to clearly expressing objectives and quantifying what it means to accomplish them, not only upstream from your team, but also downstream from upper management and sidestream to other areas of the company. Best of all, this transparency does not require that stakeholders schedule meetings, gather personnel, and present slides. On the contrary, the process is open for everyone. It is easy to identify whether OKRs, including yours, are aligned with the company's. When misaligned, it is easy to correct course. When aligned, you will know that efforts are applied as designed.

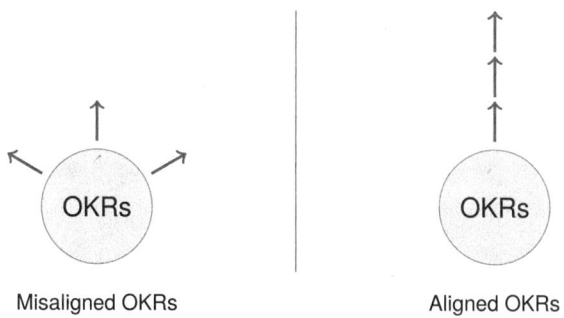

Figure 7.6: OKR Alignment.

We know that when vectors point in the same direction, their magnitude is larger than when they are misaligned, as illustrated in Figure 7.6. For instance, if stakeholders upstream plan to expand internationally, and your team only implements user interface and messages in your native language, there is a misalignment of objectives. On the other hand, you can build alignment. For instance, if your resources are stretched because you must add support to nine required languages, you can achieve this by adding support incrementally to three languages each quarter.

There is a periodic nature to OKRs, typically quarterly. Sometimes OKRs may be long-lived and span multiple quarters. Nevertheless, OKR goals should be reachable at some point and finite in scope.

Another benefit, in addition to transparency, is making you and the team accountable for attempting to reach the OKRs. Note that I did not say to achieve them but to make progress toward achieving them. Part of the spirit of OKRs is to set ambitious goals. They should be achievable but not easily. If you only get 70 percent there, that is 100 percent all right.

That is an important reason why compensation should be decoupled from OKRs. Had these two things been coupled, that would be a perverse incentive against the principle behind it. If someone's compensation is tied to achieving an OKR, during the planning period, they will draft them in such a way that it will be easy to attain. By decoupling OKRs and compensation, ambitious goals are permitted, and the team can aim for the moon.

There are two broad categories of objectives: commitment and aspirational. At the end of the period, you either accomplished the commitment or not—again, no penalty. Aspirational objectives should be a stretch in the way you challenge yourself and the team. If you are consistently accomplishing 100 percent of your objectives, this is a sign that you should plan to be more ambitious next time.

Nestled within each of the objectives are key results, and each of them can be one of the following three types:

1. **Percentage based:** Results that are better when measured using percentages, such as increasing unit tests code coverage to a minimum of 90 percent of the codebase.
2. **Value based:** Results are better measured using a numeric value. For example, users should click at most four times to get to any screen.
3. **Binary:** Results are either achieved or not. The company can obtain a security certification or not. In both cases, there is

no state in between. Even if the process is ongoing and at 99 percent, a certificate will not be issued.

The hardest part may be when you sit down to draft the OKRs. At that moment, you may feel like the writer staring at the proverbial blank page, searching for inspiration to begin. Now that we know the basics, let's put it all together with a few examples:

1. **Create engaging experiences for customers.**
   - Reduce latency time to less than 200 milliseconds.
   - User should be able to complete any task on the system by navigating no more than three pages.
   - Reduce the number of support tickets by 5 percent.
2. **Expand internationalization (I18N).**
   - Add support to three new languages.
   - All languages should be supported in at least 80 percent of the user interface.
3. **Improve alerts and monitoring.**
   - Implement a dashboard displaying at least 90 percent of the technical KPIs.
   - (Aspirational) Integrate alerts with the company's messaging system.

You should write the first draft of the OKRs and use it as a starting point to begin a conversation with your team; the product manager could help write it. This would be beneficial to the planning process because, rather than staring at a blank screen and trying to come up with ideas, a draft would provide momentum. Make the team feel welcome to debate and make suggestions, so everyone has a chance to accept, reject, add, remove, or modify the original text.

You may decide to inject a healthy dose of skepticism. Consider the words of Danish physicist Niels Bohr, known for contributing to the understanding of atomic structure and quantum theory, who remarked about forecasting: "Prediction is very difficult, especially if it's about the future."

Once you settle on the final version, share it with the whole company. There are many software solutions that offer a platform to host and track the progress of OKRs.

Once the OKRs are published, update them at regular intervals. Some key results may be updated monthly, others weekly, and in rare cases, daily. The updates are an efficient way for your team to communicate transparently with the rest of the company.

Regardless of how much effort was invested or how good the planning and the drafting of the OKRs, circumstances may change during the period, and adjustments may be necessary. Instead of charging forward toward the completion of an OKR that is no longer applicable, it is preferable to abandon it and explain the reasons. Communicate the criteria that led to this decision clearly and transparently to all stakeholders and observers of the OKR. Appropriately adapting to the circumstances is a more effective deployment of the team.

Be careful about commitments that are outside your reach and control. Assume that you manage an engineering team, and you learn from upstream OKRs that the company wants to bring ten new customers. You want to show alignment and add that objective as one of your own. Here is the problem: How can your team bring new customers? Would the engineers stop technical work and begin prospecting leads? A better commitment, equally aligned, is to ensure that the system is robust and scalable, and can safely support the new customers. Only agree to items that are within your scope or a scope to which you want to expand.

Some companies extend the adoption of OKRs all the way to individual contributors, and other companies stop at the departmental level. In my experience, team-level OKRs have been the most successful. That said, the level of granularity may be different at your organization. All the concepts we explored here are still valid; only the scale is different.

Status Updates

Status updates are a communication tool aimed at keeping stakeholders updated on the progress of projects, calling attention to areas where help is needed and keeping a detailed journal of the project.

There are two ways to deliver the updates: synchronously by hosting a meeting with slides and asynchronously by publishing a written report. A third way, where both a report and meeting are required, is also possible.

My preference, and the content of this section, focuses on asynchronous status updates, which can be easily adapted to slides. The content, in written report format, conveys the same message and is accompanied by multiple benefits:

- Recipients can read it at their convenience.
- It eliminates the need to hold meetings where everyone has to be present at the same time.
- It is a consistent presentation format facilitating understanding and highlighting topics that need attention.

The report describes the state of projects, including progress made in completing a road map, achievements, obstacles, onboarding of customers, team, engineering, product, and whatever else you deem worth mentioning.

Time the writing and the release cadence of status updates. Depending on the nature of the project, it may be appropriate to publish them on a weekly, biweekly, or monthly basis. Whatever your choice, I would recommend against going more than a quarter without publishing them.

The number of topics and length of sentences is of less importance. The most important aspect is that the message is clear to the stakeholders. It should tell the story of the project, including timelines and effort invested.

Discoverability and continuity of the status updates are fundamental aspects of it. They not only highlight the storytelling aspect, but also give openness to the process. A Wiki-like knowledge base may be one of the best places to keep the updates since the formatting is lightweight, highly portable, and can be easily read as plain text. Other options include an online, shareable document. Whichever choice is available to you, remember that the reports should be easy to find and present a clear timeline and milestones. All who read the reports should be able to understand and replay the events.

If the gap between an event and logging it into a journal is too wide, the information may become outdated or incorrect. Make a habit of taking notes in a draft document as events happen. This way, most items will have a brief description and are less likely to be forgotten, and you will have a starting point when it is time to write the actual report. Plus, you will struggle less with the writing.

Writing a status update may take longer than you imagine. The report should be concise and clear, which takes effort. Realistically speaking, budget forty-five to sixty minutes of uninterrupted time to write it.

The layout and formatting may vary. Perhaps it needs to follow a company template, or maybe you can come up with your own. Sample 7.1 shows a fictitious status update as a reference for you. The first topic is a brief compilation of noteworthy mentions containing highlights from the other topics or an item with a message of its own.

Looking back at past status updates could help you. A quarterly review, retelling the story of accomplishments, obstacles, shortcomings, and other factors will be a valuable exercise. It will also help you answer the question: "Is progress being made in the right direction?" This assessment will give you insights regarding what to start, or stop, or continue doing.

Status Update
June 1st

Topic	Description
Noteworthy	• Three new customers + one renewal. • Successful release of version 3.0. • Interviewed *Customer B* about the new version of the product.
Customer	• *Customer A* and *Customer B* signed up for a two-year contract. • *Customer D* renewed their contract for another year. • Customers were interviewed about *feature X*. It works according to their expectations, and they loved the speed at which results appear on the screen. There was one suggestion: They want to be able to export the results to a spreadsheet.

Engineering	• The new end-point API, to publish inference results, is code complete, but tests are still needed. We are working on documentation and code samples before releasing it. • ETL is now running on an hourly rather than daily basis. This was made possible by migrating to streaming the data extraction.
Product	• We want to integrate *feature Y* with a messaging system; this will allow for notifications to be tracked more easily. • The plan for next quarter is complete and will be presented to stakeholders next week in our staff meeting.
Other	• We welcomed Jannat to the team. Jannat joins us after having worked on the Flux Capacitor and the Tardis and will be helping us implement the multiplexer.

Sample 7.1: Reference Status Update.

Presentations

Presentations are an exercise in clear communication to stakeholders, the team, customers, and others. Perhaps you are giving a status update, introducing a new feature or product, or asking for resources. Whatever the case, consider the audience. What is in the update that will benefit them? Will people be attending because of the content or for the snacks in the conference room? You are the host, and a good host is a master of stepping away from the spotlight and letting their guest [the content] shine. Make the presentation worth the attendees' time.

Before you present the main content, explain the purpose, the message you expect that attendees will take away from it, or the decision that needs to be made. Then, let the audience know how long the meeting will likely take. By knowing the purpose, what is needed from them, and how much time they will be investing in the meeting, you eliminate the anxiety of unknowns and create the space for everyone to feel comfortable and focus on the meeting.

The details of the presentation are contextual; it depends on what you need to talk about. Below are some topic suggestions:

The State of the Project: Here, you want to present the mission of the project, where the project is and where it needs to go, the markets the product is addressing, and profiles of team members and why they are the right people. Let them know that some of the metrics presented here are described in the "Business Metrics" and "Technical Metrics" sections.

Competition and Market Analysis: Explain the market segments and the target audience. Lay out the product differentiators and how this product is better than the competition's product. Name a few customers and, if available, share quotes from customers testifying to the value of the product. Describe some cases of successful use.

Release the Schedule and a Road Map: Present a high-level system diagram, set expectations for the features that will be available, and show where the project is on a timeline containing feature milestones.

Demo: Show the product in action. Create a hypothetical scenario and relay how someone would use the product. This is also a great opportunity for you to share the stage with other team members. Prior to the presentation, ask them to present the demo to you or a small group of people, and allow them to rehearse. Make sure that everything will work according to the script.

Things to Remember: You and your team may have covered a substantial amount of material in the presentation. At the end, recap the topics you discussed and show a list of takeaways. This helps solidify the message and the focus points you want to highlight.

When preparing slides, resist the temptation to pack in as much content as possible. Slides are anchors for the content you are presenting, rather than reading material. By using lightweight slides including charts, figures, and little to no text in a font size no smaller than 30, attendees will pay attention to what you are presenting, rather than being distracted with reading or digesting the details of dense slides. In the event you need to include detailed content, write a companion document to the presentation, and send it in advance to attendees as recommended pre-reading material.

There may be topics or specific presentation points for which further clarification is needed. Create the space for questions by pausing for a few moments between topics or even soliciting questions from the attendees. Interaction with the audience means engagement with the topics, and that generally means the message is getting through.

If the content is longer than time allows, insert a slide containing a keywords diagram with all the topics in the presentation and point out that you selected a few of them for the conversation. Highlight the keywords you will focus on in bold, larger font size, and color. And render the other keywords in a smaller font size and a light shade of gray or dimmed color.

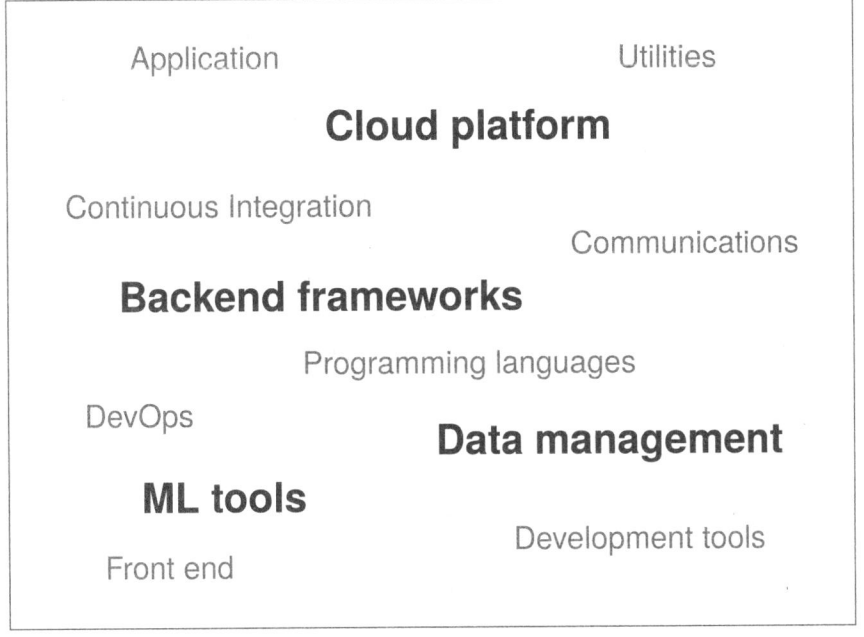

Figure 7.7: Keywords Diagram Slide.

The productivity of the meeting can be further improved when you anticipate plausible objections and discuss them before they come up in the presentation. There may be questions such as these:

- Did you consider that competitors may be doing X or Y?
- Have you evaluated tools A and B?

- Does the schedule account for time off during the holidays?
- How can we measure the gains of implementing feature Z?

By addressing these, you acknowledge their importance, you show that you are in sync with the audience, and you remove obstacles to discussing the items you shared with the attendees.

What message will attendees take with them when the presentation ends? Remember that you are speaking to people and that it is unlikely they will remember what you covered in the presentation. At the end, include a slide with the main takeaways. If participants could remember three key points, what would you want them to be?

Self-Assessment

Every now and then, it is worth pausing to reflect on your work, performance, aspirations, and fitness to your role. In addition, thinking and writing about it will help with self-promoting conversations upstream, when you can share how you are adding value to the company. This is not humblebragging. Not at all. It is a fundamental dynamic in the relationship between labor and capital. You want to be compensated fairly, and the company wants to pay according to the market. Finding this equilibrium is one of the pillars for longevity at work. Both parties see and understand the value of one another.

What other values do you gain in this dynamic? It could include satisfaction at work, accomplishments, failures (some risk-taking is necessary), a sense of belonging, fulfilling aspirations, and more. Success needs to be accompanied by a story that shows demonstrable achievements.

Note that self-assessment is an instrument of transparency, whether you are performing well, average, or suboptimally, that will become apparent to you and upstream management. If the picture does not look as good as you would like, rather than trying to embellish the evaluation, embrace the results and work on fixing your flaws going forward. Doing so will lead to much greater career satisfaction.

There are many ways to evaluate yourself at work. Keeping a journal is a great way to store your thoughts in one place for easy reference. A daily journal may be too much. I prefer to write things down only when I think they are important enough to save for later. An event may seem worth jotting down in the moment, but in hindsight, it may be unimportant. You can always delete or alter those entries.

Another way is to sit down with pencil and paper or keyboard and a new document—whatever you prefer—and start remembering major thoughts about your work. Jot down accomplishments, shortcomings (you learn from risks and failures), what you have learned, what you need to work on, how to deepen your network, how to change your scope of responsibilities, lessons learned, and other topics that may come to mind.

When writing, focus on achievements and strengths. This is about recording your competency in areas where your interest is highest and most of the value is added. Beware that you will need to share these upstream at some point in a formal self-assessment, and upstream needs to perceive your contributions as you do. If upstream views you differently, skip being upset, and take it as a lesson learned. You may think you are doing great, but you may not know enough to understand there could be shortcomings.

Most efforts to improve yourself should go toward building up your strengths. It may seem counterintuitive at first, but as discussed in "Managing Different Personality Types" and "Career Framework" in chapter 4, you should aspire to get better in areas where you perform well, rather than reach a plateau. If, instead, you put most of your effort into trying to recover from your weaknesses, you will, at best, be average at them—at the cost of not investing that time and effort into improving what you do best.

Michael Jordan's achievements are a powerful example of winning if you invest in your strengths. Jordan is among a handful of the best basketball players who ever lived, and in 2023 a poll of professional athletes across all sports voted him the best athlete of all time. In the 1990s, Jordan longed to join professional baseball, even though he hadn't played since high school. He trained fiercely and steadily improved his performance with the minor-league Birmingham Barons. Jordan ended up with a .202 batting average, well behind the rest of the Barons roster. Another way to see this would be to ask a cello player to stop practicing the strings and instead play the trumpet with the pretext of improving their skills on brass instruments. It would not make sense.

Back to our discussion of self-assessments. Note that I said most investments—not all—should focus on developing your strengths. There will be times when you will need to invest in upgrading your weaknesses to achieve at least a minimum level of proficiency. For example, you may be great technically but not so great at presentations and storytelling. It may be worth your time and effort to invest in those.

Preparing a self-assessment is an intimate moment to reflect on yourself and an opportunity for you to consider your career, your accomplishments, lessons learned, and aspirations for the future. Reserve an hour or more to work on the first draft. I prefer to work on tasks like these early in the morning before any disruptions and while the mind is fresh.

Here are a few suggestions of topics for you to consider:

- Deliveries against committed goals.
- Areas where you see a need for growth.
- New skills to develop.
- Fitness, in the sense of being suitable to fill a role.
- Enjoyable and not enjoyable aspects of the work.
- Network and belonging. How are your professional relationships at the company? What new connections would you like to make?
- Present and, if possible, future motivations.
- Scope of responsibilities. Are they too little, too much, or just right?

Be honest. List accomplishments, contributions, development of skills, failures, and investments that should not have been made. Describe how you are going to keep growing, areas of interest, and career ambitions. If you want to keep growing, include the areas where you thought growth would have happened faster or better. Evaluate your alignment with the values of your company, the mission of your team, and with what you want to do.

Even if the period you are evaluating was unfortunate, with little to show, keep a professional tone. Itemize what affected your work performance—not as a means to avoid accountability—and discuss this with your manager. Blaming circumstances, other people, the weather, or other external factors will solve nothing and prevent you from identifying and working on improving. Yes, those factors may have had an impact, but your focus should be on the things you can influence and control.

Your conversations upstream will be better when conducted in the spirit of fixing behavior going forward, rather than dodging responsibility. Discuss actionable items, and set milestones for follow-up.

Upon completing a self-assessment, you should have a better understanding of the work you do, what you do well, what areas need improvement, and a glimpse into the future. This paves the way for conversations about compensation, promotion, and career growth in general.

Plan how you are going to communicate the assessment upstream, and complete the process with a conversation with your manager and others, as needed.

Customers

Customers are the people and businesses you, your team, and your company serve. They have a problem, an inefficiency, or some other challenge, and you have a solution (or are building one) that helps them solve it better, faster, more affordably, more reliably, and so on.

The work does not stop when the product is delivered to customers. Some may say that delivering is the landmark where the real work begins. As more and more customers use your product, you will start observing shortcomings, struggles, and areas for improvement. You will also see novel ways to use it that were unimagined during development, suggestions for new use cases, and more.

Maintaining a close working relationship with your customers becomes essential to the evolution of the product. The feedback they give should be an integral part of future versions. This does not mean that you will guide all development according to customer feedback. It means their feedback must be carefully considered when deciding what to build next and planning the road map.

The skill of interviewing customers is a competence that one or more people on the team or in the company must master. It is paramount to know which questions to ask and how to dig for information that would help future development. What is the real problem you are trying to solve? Keep asking questions about the *what, how, when,* until you get to the core. Sometimes this means asking the same question in a different way or sometimes switching to a new question. This is more an art than a science, and like all arts, experience is the key differentiator. Frequent practice doing interviews is necessary to maintain the required dexterity. In addition to knowing how to interview, it is crucial that the interviewer practices it often.

A few core elements are recommended for the interviews. The following table contains suggestions of questions both for your team and your customers. The answers will give you insights for improving the product.

Ask questions to understand the context of the problem you are trying to solve and how the solution performs:
- How does the customer experience the problem?
- How often does the problem occur? Daily, hourly, continuously?
- What do they do on their own (without your tool) to solve the problem?
- What is the cost (in time, number of people, etc.) when the problem occurs?

While using your products, ask these questions before each step:
- What do you expect to accomplish with this step?
- How are you going to operate it?
- What do you think the product will do after you complete this step?

At the end of the session, ask final-thoughts questions:
- Did the product work well?
- Which parts of the product would you trust to help you in your work? Which parts wouldn't you?
- How would you pitch this product to a colleague or persuade your manager to buy it?

Sample 7.2: Questions for Customer Interviews.

As much as customers will appreciate having their voices heard and considered, constant participation in these focus group meetings may not be feasible for all of them. To accommodate those customers, consider adopting a rotation schedule. This way, the need to join is less frequent, and no one gets overwhelmed.

Observing customers while they use your product to do their work is another technique you may consider. There are cases where this may not be possible, but if it is, take advantage of the opportunity. You may either invite customers to your company and set up an environment to observe and interact with them while they use your product, or you visit them and see them in action at their location.

Although either option to observe customers using the product is good, my personal preference is to visit customers at their offices. The rationale is that having an observer is already a disturbance in their day, which may affect the accuracy of the observations. A change in their environment adds an extra variable to the equation, potentially increasing variability. It would be more difficult to assert whether the observed results were due to changes in the product.

Forming a small community of customers is likely to lead to more in-depth conversations and more engagement in the design process, giving you even more valuable feedback. This, in turn, will benefit the customers since the feature is more likely to function the way they and other customers expect. These focus groups are also likely to be, or become, your most enthusiastic early adopters.

Back in the "Demos" section of chapter 5, we discussed how presentations would progressively become more polished until they were ready to be shown to customers. During focus group meetings or with other customers, the demos will have been incrementally rehearsed and improved in quality, and now they are ready to shine. Together with the interviews, you will have information to bring back as feedback to the team and discuss if, when, and how to incorporate it into the product.

Interviewing and observing customers are just two, albeit important, kinds of interactions you may work on together. Limiting your cooperation to those, however, will only give you—and them—a partial benefit. Testing experimental features, A/B testing of different implementations of the same features, and more will help. If the interactions have a clear purpose and are worth the investment of your time and your customers' time, the insights you gain will be an important contribution to the final product.

CHAPTER 8

Managing Sidestream

Nothing in life is to be feared; it is only to be understood. Now is the time to understand more so that we may fear less.
—Marie Curie

More likely than not, you and your team collaborate with other teams, rather than working independently in a corporate vacuum. Such collaboration is necessary when dealing with many issues, from interoperability between systems via APIs to accessing persistence layers, interviews with customers, and much more. The collaboration among teams is an essential aspect to the success of your products and the company.

If we were programmable robots, relationships between teams could be reduced to purely transactional ones. We are more than that; we are humans, social animals, and as such, we need to interact for more reasons than just business concerns. There are those who insist on operating in a purely transactional manner.

On the other side of the spectrum, there is networking. It has become a term that is loaded, overused, and dreaded by many. Why is it dreadful? Many peoples' perception of the concept is a negative one. It is an activity in which one interacts superficially with other people they barely know, so they can talk about generic topics on the remote chance their professional paths will cross again.

The ingrained idea most have about networking is of an activity with ephemeral connections that are a waste of time, uncomfortable, and sometimes fake. Mercifully, we are referring here to a benign variation of networking. We are advocating networking as a regular way to meet with people with whom you share common goals and interests and with whom you wish to collaborate. The exchange of ideas, awareness of advancements being made in products, and opportunity to meet new team members—all can make a tangible impact on your day-to-day work, although it may not be immediately perceptible, unless your mind is ready to notice the benefits.

Networking also helps you build social capital. It is similar to the way a bank account works, where you make deposits and withdrawals. The currency, however, is not monetary. Here, it is trust, values, and relationships. These "currencies" give you the ability to work effectively and efficiently with others.

Robert Cialdini, who writes extensively about reciprocity in his book *Influence*, acknowledges reciprocity as a powerful human sentiment. When someone does you a favor, you feel indebted to that person and are more likely to help them if they ever need or ask for assistance. The reverse is also true. When you help someone, they feel compelled to help you back when you need it. Beware, however, that reciprocation may be disguised as uninvited debt. There may be those who do you a "favor" with the hidden agenda of making you indebted to them. A vendor may take you to a nice dinner in the hope that you will select their product; a colleague may answer a bug alert over the weekend, only to ask you to take their on-call rotation during the holidays. Those favors asked in return are usually disproportional in value, vis-à-vis the favor done for you.

Noted Congolese sociologist-anthropologist Pierre Van Den Bergh wrote in his 1978 paper, "A Socio-Biological Perspective"[3] that reciprocity "is cooperation for mutual benefit, and with expectation of return, and it can operate between kin or between non-kin."

A variation of reciprocity is concession. It takes the form of first asking for a favor that requires considerable effort, and after reluctance or

---

3   https://www.scribd.com/document/57320545/sociobiology.

refusal from your part, asking a smaller favor. You may not want to do either, but since you feel "bad" for declining the first request, you try to make up for it by agreeing to do the second ask. For example, a colleague may ask if you and your team could deploy the new version of the product. When you reply that this is not something your team is prepared to do, they may ask if you could at least prepare the slides for the presentation to stakeholders prior to the release.

Most colleagues have good intentions and are not trying to exploit reciprocation. My approach is to assume the best from everyone, unless proven otherwise. This is not only an optimistic view but also a much more productive way of maintaining relationships. If exploited by someone, that person will lose my trust immediately; however, that rarely happens. If you adopt a more pessimistic approach about people and are suspicious of most, that attitude will burn too many unnecessary mental cycles with false positives.

When you find yourself in a situation in which you detect deception or trickery, simply say "no" with a clear conscience, and remember whatever favor the other person did for you. Since the act was not sincere, that is the price they pay for trying to take advantage of you. On the other hand, for most interactions you have with colleagues, do reciprocate.

There will be times when you may need to cold-call someone or contact an old friend you haven't kept in touch with and ask for a favor. In these situations, there is little to no social capital accumulated. What should you do?

One may be tempted to reach out to the person and start building a minimum amount of social capital, right before changing the conversation and coming forward with the ask. Please do not go down this route. The person will feel betrayed and used. They will be under the impression that you were genuinely interested only to have the rug pulled out from under their trust.

As a rule, be honest and transparent. When you contact someone under those circumstances, be up-front from the start. Failing to do so may prevent you from having a second interaction with that person. Explain to them why you are beginning the conversation, what you would need from them, and how this will be worth of their time. Describe the impact their help will have on what you are trying to do. People will appreciate the honesty and transparency, and they will like the feeling that they are being useful. If you need to call again in the future for another favor, they will know what to expect from you and likely will be willing to help. You will have their trust and vice versa.

Of course, it is not necessary that you become someone's friend nor maintain a professional relationship because you asked for a favor. No one has such expectations. If, however, you find that you have interests in common, there may be a chance for a friendship, mentorship, or professional relationship. Those do not happen often; nevertheless pay attention and seize the opportunity when it presents itself.

When you meet others and listen to their interests and discuss books they are reading, conferences they took part in, or work they are developing, you may find common interests. You may want to keep in touch to share news and views. Inevitably, there will be ideas applicable to a project one of you is working on or opportunities for you to work together, perhaps, for example, with one of you being an early adopter of a new functionality.

Developing and investing in a network of peers and colleagues leads you to learn about new projects, new hires, advances in critical initiatives, or new technical or other frameworks being adopted to scale, strengthen, or reinvent parts of a company.

After you have presented a demo and need feedback, you might want to share an idea or ask for advice, or perhaps one of you is looking for a corporate sponsor to fund a project. The people in your network will likely be able to guide you through the right channels and connect you with appropriate stakeholders.

The people in your company share a larger purpose and are working toward bringing a version of its vision to reality. Communication is the precursor to action, and your message arises either from alignment or the need for alignment. Both cases are followed by doubling down on something or course correcting.

One of the biggest impacts of using networking as a strategic lever in your professional life is being informed about what matters and engaging people to accomplish the realization of a vision.

Picture a peer of yours from another team who recently attended a data management conference and is experimenting with asynchronous read-and-write to a database. They share the current state of a proto-type's implementation with you, and you and your team decide to be early adopters of the new feature. Now your product has a higher data throughput, and your peer's team has a partner for constructive feedback during the development of the product—a win-win for everyone. That is one of many ways that networking may have a direct impact on the work you do.

Taking the first step in networking often requires a nudge. If you need ideas to get started, here are a few suggestions:

- **Schedule regular individual meetings** with peers from other teams. Find out what cadence works best for each case, and make a habit of meeting and talking. Be mindful of being expansive regarding the topics you discuss; avoid limiting the conversation only to work-related topics.
- **Organize small, informal gatherings.** When a handful of people get together, conversation topics surface more easily. Feel free to rotate the participants.
- **Spread knowledge.** Host technical and product presentations about what your team has been working on. Also, invite peers to present the work of their teams. Learning the details about how products and features were built may inspire your team. When you share, other teams may be inspired, too.
- **Establish and maintain cross-team collaboration.** It is plausible to assume that your team's project and the projects of your peers have elements in common. Would it be possible to coordinate the development of a shared library, a portion of user interface, or some other component? You would be fostering collaboration and building a reusable component—two accomplishments with one action.

Although often perceived unfavorably, networking need not be fake or artificial. When a colleague comes to you and asks for help solving a problem or invites you for a walk or a cup of coffee, chances are that you will say yes. When looking at this scenario with your own eyes, you want to be helpful. Why, when imagining the same situation from the perspective of a colleague, would you see it any differently? Thus, networking establishes a two-way connection.

Expand your horizon to beyond your group within the company. Speak with folks from sales, customer support, legal, and more. They will have a lot to say about customers, the impact of products, new ideas, frustrations, positive stories of how the product is improving people's lives, and new compliance requirements that need to be implemented soon. They will be equally appreciative when you share information about new features, road maps, and bug fixes, and what customer profiles are the best fit for the product as currently implemented.

Product

Your relationship with product will be mostly in collaboration with a product manager (PM). My idealized view of a PM is someone who lives in the future and, during business hours, comes back to the present to share with the rest of us what needs to be built. They are indispensable in the correspondence with customers and in influencing the implementation of products.

This vision of the future has a tremendous impact in planning features, allocating resources, executing the road map, and choosing which tools to adopt for implementation.

Having a great relationship with your PM is a must. This does not mean you agree on everything or that their word (or yours) is final and should be followed blindly. On the contrary, the conversations between you will, at times, inevitably diverge, with each of you bringing different points of view to the table. It is only by listening to each other and understanding the other's perspectives that you will be able to address core points. Contribute to the conversation with your experience, expertise, and empathy.

PMs may ask for "crazy" and "unimaginable" requests. In fact, it is part of their job to think about and propose what may be considered the impossible. Rather than complaining and questioning the reasoning, ask the PM to explain to you where they are coming from, what the motivation is behind the idea, how that will be used by customers, and so forth. In return, share with them the effort required to implement such a feature, the technological constraints, and your perspective on the basic idea.

The reality is that both of you will be thinking under assumptions made with incomplete information. Only by talking through the details and sharing where each of you are coming from can you have a fuller view and understanding of what is being proposed and how to build it.

This cycle will be repeated again and again with each feature, proposal, or refactoring of the product. Therefore, you want to be dialectical, with both wanting to find the best outcome. Understand that cultivating rapport, trust, and respect are necessary conditions for longevity in your work relationship with the PM. Left on its own, things will begin to fall apart after the first disagreement.

It would be best if conflicts between you were few and far between. Here, conflict is defined as a situation where some issues are unresolved or where conversations between you have come down to civil niceties that avoid discussion of topics that need to be addressed.

Worse yet, there is no conversation. Differences of opinion, lack of agreement, and conflicts are inevitable. It is paramount that you talk honestly, explain where each is coming from, listen, and try to find some alignment.

Note that I did not say agreement. Cooperation with agreement is great but not necessary. Alignment, on the other hand, is a required condition for execution according to intent.

Just as you have one-on-ones with members of your team, you must have a regular meeting with your PM counterpart to discuss feature proposals, projects, resource allocation, prioritization, the road map, and more.

Scope and Skills of Product Managers

Product managers divide their attention over several disciplines, all of them related to identifying, building, and releasing products to customers. They vary from engineering to focus groups, stakeholders, and more, as depicted in Figure 8.1.

Engineering is exploded in the chart because this is usually where PMs spend most of their time. After all, that is where the product is built. Since PMs are often seen in engineering discussions, some may incorrectly assume that this is the only team with whom they collaborate and interact.

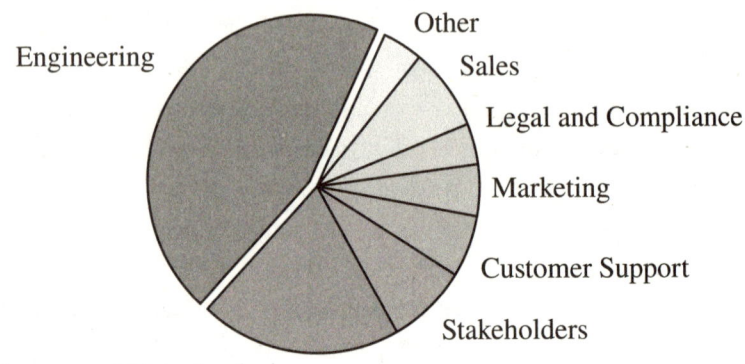

Focus Groups and Data Analysis

Figure 8.1: Rough Distribution of a PM's Attention.

Identifying pain points for customers and imagining ways to address them is one of the key contributions of a PM's work. We can define addressing a pain point as understanding why customers care about a given solution to an identified problem and how it makes products better. This requires an excellent understanding of the related workflow, otherwise your solution may be already at a disadvantage compared to competitors.

Some folks claim that product managers are akin to the CEO of a product. Although I disagree with this definition, I am using it here to illustrate why some PMs demand ownership of the product. The way I see it, PMs are stewards of the product, sharing ownership with stakeholders, but this is not always the case. There are circumstances in which a manager with technical knowledge and domain expertise may be more effective in defining what to build, in addition to how it will be built, especially in cases where the PM is inexperienced or falls short in expertise. In situations like these, the role of a PM is not diminished in any way, shape, or form. They still have a wide range of responsibilities, as seen in Figure 8.1.

Often overlooked is the role PMs play in adjudicating when the product is defined enough and implemented enough to ship. Left on their own, engineering may want to perfect it for too long, whereas sales may want to release it prematurely, and so forth. Product managers have the incentive to ship products precisely when features and timing are right—perhaps even a tad earlier.

It is widely known that product managers come from many different backgrounds. Some may have transitioned from engineering, design, or operations, and many come from a variety of origins. Irrespective of how they became product managers, there are three fundamental characteristics that determine their ability to be effective:

1. Technical expertise
2. Domain-specific knowledge
3. Excellent communication

When engineers and technicians talk to each other, they use terminology and language that is specific to the technologies used to research and develop the product. If a PM is nontechnical, other participants in the conversation need to use abstractions to facilitate understanding. This leads to loss of signal fidelity, and this becomes a communication problem since it sacrifices the integrity of the information. When generalizations are used with customers, the intent is to persuade them about the product, encapsulate complexity in a few words, and make it easier for them to understand the benefits; customers are not defining the details nor building the product. Most people can use a mouse and keyboard to interact with a graphical user interface (GUI), yet the majority would not be able to explain the details of how a GUI works. Without proper technical knowledge, PMs would participate in the periphery of conversations, unable to communicate details, which would inevitably limit their effectiveness.

Domain-specific knowledge and understanding of the principles that underpin a product are necessary to define what to implement, optimizations, and leap-forward advancements. If PMs have insufficient mastery of these, it means they must rely on outsiders to bring that knowledge to the conversation. The details of the product may become unintentionally simplified and functionality compromised. Each translation of business needs to technical specifications would lose precision.

That is a problem because implementation requires specificity.

These criteria are especially true in business-to-business companies, where customers tend to have a deep knowledge of the domain and its technical aspects.

The situation is a little more flexible in business-to-consumer companies. There, customers are motivated by different messages, such as advertisements and network effects. Nevertheless, nontechnical and nonexpert product managers should, at a minimum, have a solid understanding of the technology that is more than superficial and less than expert.

A nontechnical and nonexpert PM is far from ideal, nonetheless they can temporarily work if they have extraordinary communication skills. They would be doing customer interviews, preparing demos with the sales team, talking details with legal and compliance, and delivering presentations to stakeholders, and they would be involved in other activities that are important for the product life cycle. This should be a temporary arrangement. Make the case with upstream stakeholders that it is necessary to look for a product manager who would be a better fit.

Product stewardship entails considerable responsibilities for the following:

- Setting the product vision.
- Bringing the voice of customers to the conversation.
- Aligning the stakeholders concerning next steps.
- Defining requirements.
- Making decisions about scope and direction of the product.
- Approving or declining proposals.
- Reporting on progress, setbacks, deliverables, and timelines.

Depending on the occasion and circumstances, different team members may be better positioned to act as a surrogate owner of one or more of these responsibilities.

Ask These Questions

One of the wonderful things about working with creative people is that, at almost any moment, there is an abundance of ideas and proposals for new features and new products and the improvement of existing features and products.

Opportunities for new products will come from a variety of sources. Whatever the case, after the inception of a plausible idea that you want to pursue, there will be many follow-up conversations between you, the PM, the team, stakeholders, customers, and more. The seed stage is when it is most feasible to validate, reject, or modify a concept. It is also when experimentation is the cheapest. Several prototypes can be built to demonstrate and assess concepts.

It pays to invest time in understanding the landscape since what you learn then will have immense influence on the product's blueprint, architectural design, implementation, and so forth.

Prior to committing to building a product, find answers to the following questions:

- What problem are you trying to solve?
- Who is the target customer?
- What kind of pain points are potential customers experiencing?
- How much do customers need to have a given problem solved?
- If customers already use a solution, how does it solve that problem?
- How is the proposed solution different, and better, from alternatives in the same space?
- How will we know if the product has been successful?

Feel free to change this list to better fit your circumstances and product. For modifications you make, formulate questions to elicit a response. This will help you explore the possibilities of a product. More on this in "Deciding Whether to Build a Product" in chapter 7.

Product-Market Fit

One can be too optimistic and believe that there is product-market fit when there is not. It is then possible to be deceived by it. Here are a few scenarios illustrating how product-market fit may not yet have been achieved.

You got the concept of your project and budget approved by senior management prior to building a prototype or discussing the concept with a few trusted customers or a focus group. After that, you switch to process building and forgo continued focus on customers and product.

The product was not built for scale and is breaking with usage. It may be the software, operations, or the infrastructure.

Graphs have flatlined, you are missing estimates, you changed KPIs (e.g., from monthly revenue to monthly usage), and everyone is coming up with reasons why that is okay.

You turn your manager and stakeholders into your boss, doing what they tell you to do. Conversations with them and listening to their opinion is important, and you should consider their advice. The decision of what to do, however, is supposed to be yours. The problem with letting yourself being bossed around is that it leads to fear and self-doubt; that destroys the confidence you need to make good decisions. Rather than basing decisions on what is right for the project, you make your decisions based on what will most please your manager and stakeholders.

The lack of regularly interacting with customers in some way might lead to failed product-market fit. If you don't understand your market—your customers—and what your market wants or needs, how will your product succeed?

Likewise, lack of originality in the product and your planned features can just as well lead to failed product-market fit. Ask yourself if the product is a copy of what others are doing, or are you building something with its own identity? It is inevitable that some features may overlap in functionality with competing products. For instance, most camera apps have a shutter button. Determine what is unique about your product. How do you expect the product to be successful?

You should be able to answer no to all the following questions:

- Is your product average and still classed among top players? (Average is not enough.)
- Does the team and product lack numerical goals?
- Do you ignore the signs of lack of progress?
- Did the team stop learning about customers' preferences, technological advancements, or how the product should work?
- Are you blaming outside factors? (Success comes in part by being extraordinary.)

The pace of product development may be anything but slow. Depending on where you are relative to the maturity of the product, your pace of development may vary. An early-stage product needs a faster implementation pace to create a functioning prototype and to find product-market fit. A mature product needs a sustainable and steady pace of development. In all cases, there should always be a continuous process to decide what to build and decide on a measurement of progress.

There are many methodologies—Agile and Waterfall, for example—that may best fit the needs of your team and project. The essential consideration is that there are processes in place to help decide what to build, establish deadlines, formalize specifications (conversations alone do not count; specs must be written down), and have measurable milestones leading toward goals.

Avoid the accumulation of half-done features. This may happen for several reasons, but it is often caused by a lack of focus or trying to implement multiple different features at once. You may have the misleading impression that you have made progress, but you have nothing to show and nothing to ship to customers.

Another common reason is stopping the development of a feature midway to switch to another one because of a conversation with a customer, a suggestion from a stakeholder, or an urgent request. Avoid those situations as much as possible. It is better to direct efforts into a smaller number of features and complete their implementation. The payoff is that you will have a product to ship and higher team morale.

Investor Andy Rachleff is credited with coining the term product-market fit. In essence, he says that product-market fit is achieved when you find a group of customers who are desperate for your product or service. According to Rachleff, you start with a great product, then try to find its best market. Any robust market will not do; in fact, your product could fail there. It must be the market that is best suited to your product.

The litmus test might be this: If you discontinued your product or stopped your service, would customers be worse off? Would they lose productivity, need to find an alternative as soon as possible, or try to develop an in-house solution?

The process of finding product-market fit involves many stages, from developing your product or service to finding a small and enthusiastic group of early adopters, avoiding deceiving yourself with false impressions, and scaling to a large enough number of customers.

Managing Expectations, Accountability, and Success

Stakeholders and upstream management will have expectations on product, features, timeline, and so on. Rather than letting the project and team be adrift on a constant change of opinions and feedback coming from all directions, a better strategy is to proactively manage why *this* is what needs to be worked on, how it will be developed, and when it will be delivered. In other words, manage expectations, scope your accountability, and define success.

Moving a structural concrete pillar after standing up a building is a nearly impossible task, yet this is what it feels like to work on a project where expectations, deliverables, priorities, and expectations are constantly changing.

Your influence will be strongest at the beginning and the end of a cycle—typically a quarter of a year. At the beginning of a quarter, you publish a plan for the next three months, and at the end of the quarter you publish a retrospective with what was accomplished, the people who worked on what, plans that were canceled, course adjustments, and other noteworthy mentions.

Although these documents are used to manage upstream, this is a task you will partner with and complete with the PM.

Every company has a power structure, and it would be naive to deny its existence (see "Is This a Democracy?" In chapter 4). If you are not proactively managing expectations, and a conversation comes down to "they" said versus "we" said, chances are that "they" will prevail. In most cases, this is the correct outcome. Leaders upstream operate at a different level of autonomy, have more context, more responsibilities, and information you may not have access to. When you share planning and retrospective documents upstream, they will be able to evaluate the content, assess alignment, provide feedback, and request adjustments.

Another benefit of these documents is that you are now part of the conversation, rather than having your priorities dictated top-down. You will have the chance to learn strategy, planning, and operations from senior leaders, improving your odds of professional growth in the future.

Planning

The plan could be a simple spreadsheet listing macro tasks, milestones, and the resources assigned to each of them; it could be a descriptive document with a detailed breakdown or a combination of both. Whichever the case, keep it as simple as possible for your situation—plans change, after all. You don't want to invest a large amount of time meticulously planning something, only to have reality "disagree" with it. Plans, above all, are communication of intent. A cell on a spreadsheet or a paragraph on a document can't warp space and time to fit its will.

ETL				
Data extraction	Jan-02	Jan-31	Finley	
Pre-Processor				
Data cleanup and conversion to data frames	Jan-10	Feb-07	Abayomi	
Inference				
Anomaly detection model	Feb-01	Mar-10	Taylor	
Frontend				
Present warnings in the website	Mar-01	Mar-31	Peyton	
Present warnings in the mobile app	Feb-22	Mar-31	Jannat	

Sample 8.1: Simple Planning Spreadsheet.

Work together with the PM to draft the first version of the planning proposal and then share it with the rest of the team and include them in the conversation to complete it. Discuss the commitments and aspirations for the quarter, what is possible, and what is a stretch; whichever the case, they must be realistic since you want people to be onboard. Besides, accountability against impractical and improbable plans only lead to frustration and burnout.

Retrospective

Retrospective reports serve multiple purposes. They tell a short story of what happened during the quarter, give visibility to all readers into what was done and who were doing the work, show alignment or divergence with the plan, and explain changes in direction and pivots.

The report should be brief, containing one or two paragraphs per project or task. The idea is to communicate at a high level and leave the door open for conversations in case someone has a question or wants to know more about a specific topic.

Retrospective Report
In the previous quarter the team built the core components of Widget AI and delivered on all commitments, including the key and challenging data cleanup process that is necessary for training the anomaly detection model.

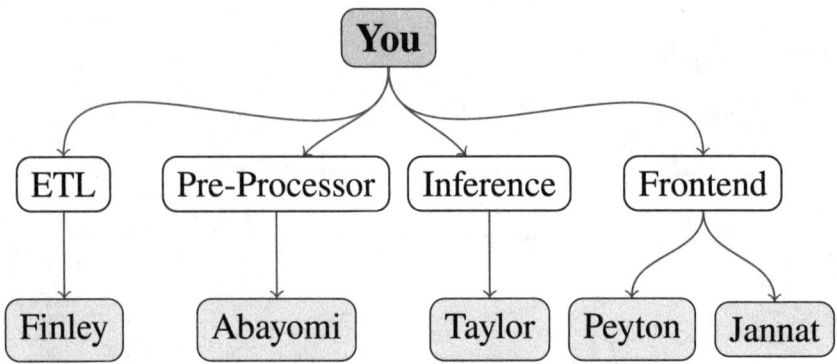

Figure 8.2: Projects and Teams.

Extract, Transform, Load (ETL)
The ETL fetches data from the database, transforms it from relational to tabular format, and loads the records to the data lake. The implementation is smart enough to identify periods of low usage and run the job during those periods.

Preprocessor
Data validation was a difficult task. Missing fields, incorrect inputs, and invalid values were among the challenges. The final implementation accounts for all known use cases and falls back gracefully in the event of an exception.

Inference
Experiments were done with different model architectures (e.g., K-Nearest Neighbors, Logistics Regression) before settling with

Gradient Boosting. The results have a great balance between precision and recall.

Front End

When entering data, users of the system will receive a warning if an anomaly has been detected. An anomaly means something uncommon, rather than necessarily an error. Users will have the chance to review the data before confirming or correcting the input.

Sample 8.2: Sample Retrospective Report.

This visibility is an additional barometer for when considering someone for a promotion or managing individual performance issues.

Protecting Intellectual Property

Your company most likely wants to avoid finding itself in a situation where it must pay to use a product it has created. Yet, this is a real possibility. Patent law in many places allows that to happen. A competitor may try to slow down your progress or a nonpracticing entity may seek to obtain compensation for licensing patents in their portfolio.

If you find yourself in such situations, your company's legal team may be able to successfully file a motion to dismiss the patent in question or even nullify it. But the litigation will be expensive and time-consuming. This is time and money that could have been better spent building products.

Instead, start a conversation with your counterparts on the legal team and develop a defensive strategy to protect services, features, and technologies implemented in your company. There are many options to consider, including patents, disclosure of inventions, publication under an open license, and more. You and your company's legal team must decide the best approach for each situation. It is common to have strategies with more than one approach, depending on the context. Rarely is there a one-size-fits-all solution.

Whatever strategies are adopted, the main goal is to avoid leaving your company in a position where the outcome of litigation forces it to pay to use something one of its own teams has created.

Patents may offer a stronger shield for protection against litigation, but they can be costly, and granting a patent can take a long time. Besides, there are no guarantees that the patent office will grant you a patent for your claims; by the same token, your patent request might be denied.

There are alternatives if patents are not an option for you. For instance, a widely adopted practice by tech companies is to establish or join a consortium with an open standard and require that vendors doing business with them be compliant with those specifications. The Open Compute Project Foundation defines and evolves hardware-related specifications. Suppliers of compliant hardware are unable to litigate with customers or competitors. This also avoids locked-in dependency on one company.

Another option could be a variation of a practice adopted by IBM between 1958 and 1998. The company regularly published a "Technical Disclosure Bulletin." Those were disclosures of inventions that IBM scientists had invented but for which IBM did not want to bear the expense of patenting; at the same time, the company did not want competitors or nonpracticing entities to obtain patents on these developments. IBM was practicing a defensive form of publishing designed to protect the company's intellectual property. Others could use the technologies described in these bulletins without having to pay IBM, but they could not use them in litigation against the company.

Patent law in the United States changed in 2011 from "first to invent" to "first inventor to file." In essence, this means that even if you published prior art but did not file for a patent, someone else could theoretically file for a patent using the content of your work—up to twelve months after it has been made available to the public. As an alternative, a provisional patent can be filed. Then, after twelve months you have the option to move forward with the patent application or let it expire. If you choose the latter, this recourse is more affordable and may have the same effect as IBM's bulletins.

There are cases of real patent infringement, but a large number of cases are filed by nonpracticing entities leveraging the power of the courts for what feels like legalized extortion. Although they do not provide any service or create any product, their business model is to use their patent portfolio to threaten legal action against companies that allegedly infringe on them.

Whichever strategy you adopt, don't try to do it alone or independently. It is in your best interest and your company's to collaborate closely with the legal team to define the best approach for you.

Afterword

There are a vast number of books about management. I noticed that many of them, if not most, share one attribute in common: the impossibility of putting into practice what is on their pages. The authors tell stories, real or fictional, that are analogies, metaphors, or anecdotes related to points they are trying to make. Good stories are inspiring and are great for motivation. They illustrate a subject, but seeing any similarity between those tales and real life requires that readers have prior knowledge of the topic. Take away the stories and those books become much shorter. I deliberately avoided such tales and analogies in this book because they do not carry explanatory knowledge, and without those, a reader will find it difficult to translate the moral of stories to their own domains.

Why can so few people, if any, realistically follow the advice or implement the frameworks in those books successfully? Authors propose and ask for almost superhuman discipline and adherence to ideal processes that are not sustainable in the long run by most professionals. The authors give advice and propose habits, routines, and mental models, many of which they themselves either cannot or do not follow.

Yes, their words are compelling and make sense to readers. We want to believe in their idealized visions; however, after one tries to put all that knowledge into practice, we reach a wall of inevitable frustration amid the thought "I may not be good enough for the job." What is proposed is that you become a romanticized quintessential manager. If you are not able to be that person and cannot make the nearly impossible happen, it is your fault. Why? Because you did not follow all the minute details of their recipe precisely.

Even if that were feasible for a few incredibly gifted and hard-working professionals, where and how would you find those people? The probability of (1) encountering such people and (2) recruiting them is incredibly small. Those managers would, quite rightly, demand a premium price for their talents.

To put this into perspective, imagine that an ideal manager would need to master n different skills ($skill_1$, $skill_2$, . . ., $skill_n$). Now consider the probability of a given manager having at least one of those skills. Let's represent those probabilities as x_{skill} (x_1, x_2, . . ., x_n). The chances of finding a manager who has all those skills is the product of all those probabilities combined:

$$p = \prod_{i=1}^{n} x_i$$

which expands to

$$p = x_1 \times x_2 \times \ldots \times x_n$$

As a thought exercise, if a manager needs to have five skills and only one in ten managers has one of those skills, we have the following probabilities: $skill_1 = 10\%$, $skill_2 = 10\%$, $skill_3 = 10\%$, $skill_4 = 10\%$, $skill_5 = 10\%$. Therefore, the chances of finding an exceptional manager with all those skills is:

$$p = 10\% \times 10\% \times 10\% \times 10\% \times 10\%$$
$$p = 0.001\%$$

Although it is not impossible to find such professionals, the chances of doing so are astonishingly small. Given that a company may need more than one manager on its staff and that many more than just one company is operating in the marketplace, the search for talent is a steep uphill battle.

In the end, there are no tools, frameworks, or techniques of management that can perform magic. You need to care, be human, and be there together with your team.

Choosing which of these processes to adopt is dependent on the size and maturity of a company. For example, a startup needs speed to move faster than others in its space and flexibility to run experiments to validate any thesis. In contrast, a larger and more established company leans toward stability and predictability for incremental evolution without breaking existing product offers.

You may agree with the contents of this book, or you may disagree with certain points. Feel free to adapt it to the reality and needs of your company. If the changes that you propose are better and are accompanied by a hard-to-vary explanation to support your argument, please share it with me. I may adopt it myself.

What was presented in this book is by no means the final word on management. The book does not propose dogmatic truth. To the contrary, what you found here were my conjectures, my best explanation of what is good, essential management, and it is meant to keep evolving to reflect and adjust to new circumstances.

Whether you want to transition to a management position, are already a manager who wants to improve your skills and effectiveness, or are a company that wants to invest in your managers to improve their performance, this book provides the tools, frameworks, operational models, and knowledge to help the majority of professionals on this planet learn, understand, and put into practice the essence of management and people leadership.

If this book has contributed to your thinking and had a positive influence on how you manage, then it has succeeded in its mission.

Sustainable Productivity Velocity

This appendix shows the technical details, equations, and the methodology used to conduct the research, analyze the data, and present the results that led to the creation of the sustainable productivity velocity framework.

As discussed on "Sustainable Productivity Velocity" in chapter 4, between 2018 and 2019, I studied the impact interruptions have on productivity. Interruptions can include unnecessary meetings, unexpected context switching (shifting from one task to another), and system failures as a result of technical debt (the result of prioritizing shortcuts over craftsmanship). All of those negatively affect the production capacity of a team, and although we all have our opinions and suspicions about how much or to what extent productivity is affected, these are just our opinions, our gut feeling, most likely not supported by data. Therefore, we avoid trying to regain that lost productivity.

Given that interruptions can be of two natures, planned (stand-up meeting) or unpredictable (service disruption), I use the word "incident" to represent interruptions, regardless of their nature.

During the study, there were 270 incidents observed over a period of ninety-one days; fifty-eight (63.74 percent) of those days experienced incidents, and thirty-three (36.26 percent) days did not. There were several different kinds of alerts triggered. They have been classified into fourteen categories and compiled in Table 9.1. (The incident names have been changed to generic names following the pattern: *Incident XX*.)

	Number of incidents	Average number of incidents per day	One incident every t hours
Incident 1	55	0.6044	39.7091
Incident 2	48	0.5275	45.5000
Incident 3	42	0.4615	52.0000
Incident 4	42	0.4615	52.0000
Incident 5	27	0.2967	80.8889
Incident 6	13	0.1429	168.0000
Incident 7	12	0.1319	182.0000
Incident 8	12	0.1319	182.0000
Incident 9	7	0.0769	312.0000
Incident 10	6	0.0659	364.0000
Incident 11	2	0.0220	1,092.0000
Incident 12	2	0.0220	1,092.0000
Incident 13	1	0.0110	2,184.0000
Incident 14	1	0.0110	2,184.0000
Total	**270**	**2.9670**	**8.0889**

Table 9.1: Incidents Statistics.

We will use a few equations to introduce mathematical rigor to the argument presented here. Try to follow the idea, even if math is not your favorite subject. The findings are accessible, irrespective of the palatability of the equations.

The first column of Table 9.1 is self-explanatory. The second and third columns are computed using equations 9.5 and 9.7. (24 is the number of hours in a day.)

$$N_I = \text{Number of incidents} \qquad (9.1)$$

$$\overline{I_d} = \frac{N_I}{24} \qquad (9.2)$$

$$\overline{I_t} = \frac{24}{\overline{I_d}} \qquad (9.3)$$

One of the properties of the data is that incidents are mostly independent from one another. By that I mean that an interruption caused by a system outage is independent from an interruption to attend a meeting to hear from a guest speaker. However, there may be correlated interruptions, such as a postmortem meeting following a system outage.

Table 9.2 shows the expected number of incidents to happen in a given number of days, based on the historical observations. For example, it is expected that "Incident 1" will happen an average of 18.1319 times within a period of thirty days.

	1	2	4	7	30
Incident 1	0.6044	1.2088	2.4176	4.2308	18.1319
Incident 2	0.5275	1.0549	2.1099	3.6923	15.8242
Incident 3	0.4615	0.9231	1.8462	3.2308	13.8462
Incident 4	0.4615	0.9231	1.8462	3.2308	13.8462
Incident 5	0.2967	0.5934	1.1868	2.0769	8.9011
Incident 6	0.1429	0.2857	0.5714	1.0000	4.2857
Incident 7	0.1319	0.2637	0.5275	0.9231	3.9560
Incident 8	0.1319	0.2637	0.5275	0.9231	3.9560
Incident 9	0.0769	0.1538	0.3077	0.5385	2.3077
Incident 10	0.0659	0.1319	0.2637	0.4615	1.9780
Incident 11	0.0220	0.0440	0.0879	0.1538	0.6593
Incident 12	0.0220	0.0440	0.0879	0.1538	0.6593
Incident 13	0.0110	0.0220	0.0440	0.0769	0.3297
Incident 14	0.0110	0.0220	0.0440	0.0769	0.3297
Total	**2.9670**	**5.9341**	**11.8681**	**20.7692**	**89.0110**

Table 9.2: Expected Number of Incidents per Day.

Each cell was computed using Equation 9.4.

$$E(I) = \frac{24}{I_t} \times d \qquad (9.4)$$

The probability of observing an incident, given an amount of time, can be modeled using a Poisson distribution. Equation 9.5 shows how the computation of probabilities was done for the data presented in Table 9.3.

$$P(k \text{ incidents per day}) = \frac{\lambda^k e^{-\lambda}}{k!} \qquad (9.5)$$

Where λ is given by Equation 9.6

$$\lambda = \frac{24}{d} \times \overline{I_d} \qquad (9.6)$$

In Table 9.3 we see the results from the modeled probability of incidents happening within a number of days (column header).

	1	2	4	6	8	10
Incident 1	3.30E-01	9.98E-02	3.04E-03	3.70E-05	2.41E-07	9.79E-10
Incident 2	3.11E-01	8.21E-02	1.90E-03	1.77E-05	8.77E-08	2.71E-10
Incident 3	2.91E-01	6.71E-02	1.19E-03	8.46E-06	3.22E-08	7.62E-11
Incident 4	2.91E-01	6.71E-02	1.19E-03	8.46E-06	3.22E-08	7.62E-11
Incident 5	2.21E-01	3.27E-02	2.40E-04	7.04E-07	1.11E-09	1.08E-12
Incident 6	1.24E-01	8.85E-03	1.50E-05	1.02E-08	3.73E-12	8.46E-16
Incident 7	1.16E-01	7.62E-03	1.10E-05	6.40E-09	1.99E-12	3.84E-16
Incident 8	1.16E-01	7.62E-03	1.10E-05	6.40E-09	1.99E-12	3.84E-16
Incident 9	7.12E-02	2.74E-03	1.35E-06	2.66E-10	2.82E-14	1.85E-18
Incident 10	6.17E-02	2.03E-03	7.37E-07	1.07E-10	8.29E-15	4.01E-19
Incident 11	2.15E-02	2.36E-04	9.51E-09	1.53E-13	1.32E-18	7.09E-24
Incident 12	2.15E-02	2.36E-04	9.51E-09	1.53E-13	1.32E-18	7.09E-24
Incident 13	1.09E-02	5.97E-05	6.01E-10	2.42E-15	5.22E-21	7.00E-27
Incident 14	1.09E-02	5.97E-05	6.01E-10	2.42E-15	5.22E-21	7.00E-27
Total	**1.53E-01**	**2.26E-01**	**1.66E-01**	**4.88E-02**	**7.66E-03**	**7.50E-04**

Table 9.3: Probability of Observing k Incidents in a Day.

The shape of the data can be better seen plotted in Figure 9.1, as we see that the probability of two incidents happening in a day is almost 25 percent. This means that focusing on a task is especially hard, due to the constant possibility of being interrupted by an incident.

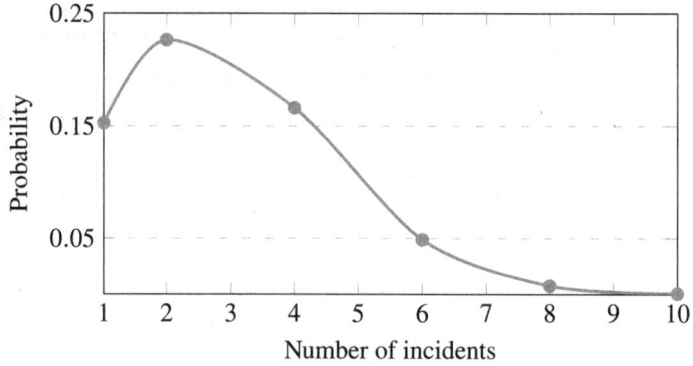

Figure 9.1: Probability of Observing k Incidents in One Day.

Here is another way of looking at this to understand the severity of the situation. Let's calculate the probability of how much time one waits until an incident happens.

	0.25	0.50	0.75	1.00	1.25	1.50	1.75	2.00
Incident 1	0.8598	0.7392	0.6355	0.5464	0.4698	0.4039	0.3473	0.2986
Incident 2	0.8765	0.7682	0.6733	0.5901	0.5172	0.4533	0.3973	0.3482
Incident 3	0.8910	0.7939	0.7074	0.6303	0.5616	0.5004	0.4459	0.3973
Incident 4	0.8910	0.7939	0.7074	0.6303	0.5616	0.5004	0.4459	0.3973
Incident 5	0.9285	0.8621	0.8005	0.7433	0.6901	0.6408	0.5950	0.5524
Incident 6	0.9649	0.9311	0.8984	0.8669	0.8365	0.8071	0.7788	0.7515
Incident 7	0.9676	0.9362	0.9058	0.8765	0.8480	0.8205	0.7939	0.7682
Incident 8	0.9676	0.9362	0.9058	0.8765	0.8480	0.8205	0.7939	0.7682
Incident 9	0.9810	0.9623	0.9439	0.9260	0.9083	0.8910	0.8741	0.8574
Incident 10	0.9837	0.9676	0.9518	0.9362	0.9209	0.9058	0.8910	0.8765
Incident 11	0.9945	0.9891	0.9837	0.9783	0.9729	0.9676	0.9623	0.9570
Incident 12	0.9945	0.9891	0.9837	0.9783	0.9729	0.9676	0.9623	0.9570
Incident 13	0.9973	0.9945	0.9918	0.9891	0.9864	0.9837	0.9810	0.9783
Incident 14	0.9973	0.9945	0.9918	0.9891	0.9864	0.9837	0.9810	0.9783
Total	**0.4763**	**0.2268**	**0.1080**	**0.0515**	**0.0245**	**0.0117**	**0.0056**	**0.0026**

Table 9.4: Probability of Waiting More than t Days until an Incident Happens.

$$P(\text{wait} < t) = e^{-\lambda t} \qquad (9.7)$$

The results in Table 9.4 were computed using Equation 9.7. There, t represents time expressed in days, and a whole day is represented by setting $t = 1$. Half a day is represented by $t = 0.5$ and so forth.

We can see by visualizing the data in Figure 9.2 that the probability of having an incident-free morning ($t = 0.5$) is smaller than 30 percent.

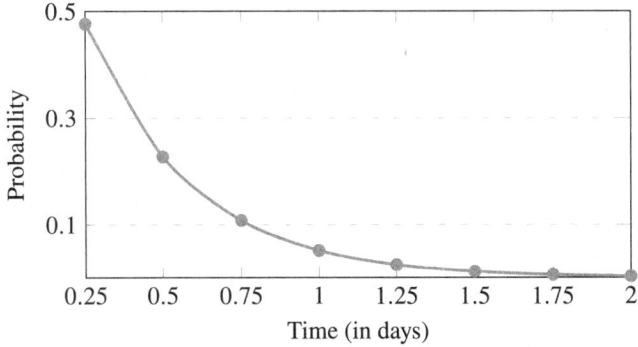

Figure 9.2: Probability of Waiting More than t Days for an Incident

You can see a theme emerging here. The more is done to avoid incidents, the more the team's productive capacity increases. Good architectural design, quality code, test coverage, timing of meetings to allow for large, and uninterrupted blocks of productive time—all of those contribute to higher output and happier teams.

The following is an exercise where three different scenarios are created with a progressive increase in the number of incidents, and for each of them, we will measure and analyze the impact that the incidents have on the productivity of a team.

Assume a standard Agile two-week sprint with epics, tasks, standups (short daily meetings to discuss progress and identify blockers), and everything else that comes with it. You can see on Table 9.5 the variables that we want to use to measure and analyze the impact of incidents, together with each of the scenarios. The argument being constructed here is about the impact to undermine productivity, not the details of the data.

Scenario 1 is the baseline with a reasonably sized team. Then, in each subsequent scenario, the parameters are relaxed to simulate the different degrees of impact on productivity from having more people on the team, more time, and fewer incidents. (We will see that adding more resources is an expensive and ineffective way of increasing productivity.)

	Scenario 1	Scenario 2	Scenario 3
Number of engineers (n)	10	12	16
Hours in a day (d)	8	8	8
Time, in hours, to solve an incident (h)	2.0	1.0	0.5
Expected number of incidents per day (i)	2.9670	2.9670	2.9670
Expected hours per day spent fixing incidents (s)	5.9341	2.9670	1.4835
Expected percentage of a day spent fixing incidents (w)	74.18%	37.09%	18.54%
Overall impact of incidents on the team (u) (distributed evenly among team members)	7.42%	3.09%	1.16%

Table 9.5: Impact Statistics.

Note that each line item has a corresponding variable enclosed in parenthesis. Those are used in Equations 9.8, 9.9, and 9.10 for the calculations of the computed fields (the bottom three rows) in Table 9.5.

$$s = h \times i \tag{9.8}$$

$$w = \frac{s}{d} \tag{9.9}$$

$$u = \frac{w}{n} \tag{9.10}$$

After the start of an Agile sprint, we want to measure the decay in productivity caused by incidents. Over time, we want to observe the cumulative impact on the team and, to some extent, the entire company.

Here, we introduce the concept of productivity velocity V. In physics, velocity is defined and measured as a change in distance over time. In the context of productivity, velocity is the change in progress building a product over time.

Equation 9.11 represents the fractional change in productivity velocity. The constant of proportionality u (Equation 9.10) is the factor by which the velocity decays over time, due to incidents impacting the productivity of the team.

$$\frac{dV}{V} = -u \, dt \tag{9.11}$$

Equation 9.11 is also an example of a differential equation. It relates the differential velocity dV to the velocity V itself and to the differential of the elapsed time dt. Integrating both sides of the equation and developing the solution gives us the following:

$$\int \frac{1}{V} dV = \int -u \, dt$$

$$\ln\left(\frac{V(t)}{V_0}\right) = -u \, t$$

$$V(t) = V_0 \, e^{-u t} \tag{9.12}$$

Where V_0, in Equation 9.12 is the initial productivity velocity, we can assume a starting value of 1 for V_0 because at the very beginning, the productivity capacity is 100 percent (no incidents yet). If, however, you have an ongoing sprint history and points assigned to each task, then V_0 would be equal to the average of all the points scheduled for a sprint, as shown in Equation 9.13. (It cannot be the points complete per sprint, as those were already subject to the impact of incidents.)

$$V_0 = \frac{1}{m} \sum_1^m S_i \qquad (9.13)$$

We use Equation 9.12 to compute each scenario in Table 9.6. Looking at how those numbers decay, we can already begin to understand how incidents can severely impact a team; the loss of productivity progresses at exponential rates.

Day	Absence of incidents	Scenario 1	Scenario 2	Scenario 3
1	100%	100.00%	100.00%	100.00%
2	100%	92.85%	96.96%	98.85%
3	100%	86.21%	94.01%	97.71%
4	100%	80.05%	91.14%	96.58%
5	100%	74.33%	88.37%	95.47%
6	100%	69.01%	85.68%	94.37%
7	100%	64.08%	83.07%	93.28%
8	100%	59.50%	80.55%	92.21%
9	100%	55.24%	78.09%	91.14%
10	100%	51.29%	75.72%	90.09%

Table 9.6: Diminishing Capacity to Work in a Sprint.

It becomes even more apparent when we plot the data in Figure 9.3. The impact incidents have is devastating to the productivity of a team. For instance, in scenario 1 the productivity is cut by almost half at the end of the sprint. And in scenarios 2 and 3, although the teams are larger, the impact is all the same. Sooner or later, their productivity will also grind to a halt.

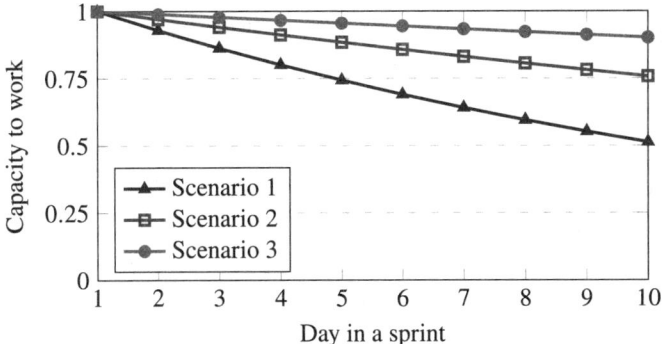

Figure 9.3: Capacity to Work in a Sprint.

It becomes clear that investing in preventing incidents is the most effective way of maintaining the productivity of a team.

The productivity of an engineer, and of a team, is directly proportional (strongly correlated) to the amount of uninterrupted time dedicated to working on tasks. Intuitively, that makes sense, but how do we quantify it? One way to do it is by asking the question: "How long does it take to complete a sprint point?" This is how we can estimate it.

$$D_g = \frac{\gamma_g}{\mu_g\left(\mu_g - \gamma_g\right)} \qquad (9.14)$$

The variables and respective indexes in Equation 9.14 are defined as the following:

g: Is an index representing a given engineer.
γ_g: Number of planned points for the sprint for engineer *g*.
μ_g: Average number of points delivered over the past *q* sprints for engineer *g*. It is suggested to use *g* = 6 as a consistency factor for deliverables over the previous quarter.

$$\text{quarter}\left(\frac{52 \text{ weeks}}{4 \text{ quarters} \times 2 \text{ weeks in a sprint}} = 6.5 \text{ sprints per quarter}\right).$$

D_g: Expected portion of a day needed for engineer g to complete a sprint point.

Let's work a practical example. Imagine that over the past six sprints Blake has delivered an average of fifteen points per sprint. During planning, Blake committed to thirteen points for the upcoming sprint. How long should it take for Blake to complete a sprint point?

$$g = \text{Blake}$$

$$\gamma_{Blake} = 13$$

$$\mu_{Blake} = 15$$

$$D_{Blake} = \frac{13}{15\,(15 - 13)}$$

$$D_{Blake} = 0.4333$$

According to the estimate, it would take Blake about 43 percent of a day to complete a single sprint point. At this rate, about two points would take about 86 percent of Blake's day, leaving 14 percent of the day for other activities. Those other activities would be best if scheduled at the beginning or end of the day (or at least before or after a lunch break) to allow for large blocks of uninterrupted time. Any other scheduling would have a direct and negative impact on productivity.

When someone is interrupted, the loss of productivity is immediate. Regaining momentum, however, takes a while. This dynamic of loss and regaining of productivity can be seen represented in Figure 9.4. Assuming that productivity is at its peak in the time range between 0 and 2, we can imagine that if an incident occurs at point 2, it will cause complete loss of velocity. The time between points 3 and 4 is an estimate of how long it takes to address the incident.

When resuming work, productivity is not restored immediately, it takes some time for one to get back to the mental state prior to the incident and regain the same level of productivity. This recovery period is represented by the sigmoid function plotted in the interval between 4 and 14. (The sigmoid function has a characteristic S-shaped curve, here meaning the acceleration period to resume full productivity.)

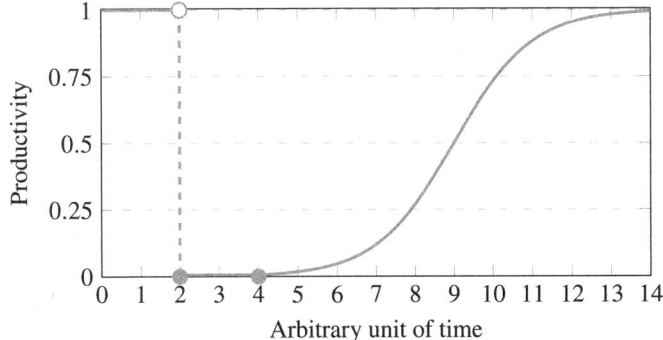

Figure 9.4: Resuming Productivity.

The time intervals in Figure 9.4 are for illustration purposes and are not plotted to scale.

In real life, the effects observed are less severe. Mercifully, unproductive meetings come to an end, the scope of features is limited, and issues are resolved relatively quickly, allowing for productivity to be restored.

Fewer incidents bring an increase in velocity, simply by freeing time that would otherwise be spent in an unproductive manner. Your team alone will not be able to take action to minimize those incidents. Often, they may feel bad (guilty) for not joining a meeting or not switching context to work on a random task when asked. You, the manager, are likely the only person in a position to act; therefore you must lead and put a deliberate effort into creating the circumstances where the team can maintain a sustainably high productivity velocity. Establish a policy that it is okay to question the need to attend certain meetings, ask for some conversations to be scheduled in advance, and to direct whoever asked them to switch tasks to first speak with you.

Sustainable productivity velocity teaches us that, to the extent possible, unwanted, unsolicited, unexpected, and burdensome distractions add severe friction to productivity. It is unrealistic and even undesirable to operate at 100 percent all the time; that only by truly understanding the costs of incidents can you make conscious trade-offs, including deliberate moments of downtime to rest and to have fun.

References and Further Reading

[1] William Bridges and Susan Bridges, *Transitions: Making Sense of Life's Changes*, reprint ed. Da Capo Lifelong Books, December 2019.

[2] Robert Cialdini, *Influence: The Psychology of Persuasion*, revised ed. Harper Business, 2006.

[3] W. Edwards Deming, *The Essential Deming: Leadership Principles from the Father of Quality*. McGraw-Hill Education, 2012.

[4] David Deutsch, *The Beginning of Infinity: Explanations That Transform the World*, reprint ed. Penguin Books, 2012.

[5] John Doerr, *Measure What Matters: How Google, Bono, and the Gates Foundation Rock the World with OKRs*. Portfolio, 2018.

[6] Peter Drucker, *The Effective Executive: The Definitive Guide to Getting the Right Things Done*, revised ed. Harper Business, 2006.

[7] Annie Duke, *How to Decide: Simple Tools for Making Better Choices*, illustrated ed. Portfolio, 2020.

[8] W. T. Gallwey, *The Inner Game of Tennis: The Classic Guide to the Mental Side of Peak Performance*, revised ed., Random House, 1997.

[9] Andrew Grove, *High Output Management*, 2nd ed., Vintage, 1995.

[10] E. T. Jaynes, *Probability Theory: The Logic of Science*, 1st ed. Cambridge University Press, 2003.

[11] Ken Kocienda, *Creative Selection: Inside Apple's Design Process During the Golden Age of Steve Jobs*. St. Martin's Press, 2018.

[12] Patty McCord, *Powerful*, 1st ed., Silicon Guild (Ingram), 2020.

[13] Karl Popper, *Conjectures and Refutations: The Growth of Scientific Knowledge*, Hassell Street Press, 2021.

[14] Jeff Sutherland and J. J. Sutherland, *Scrum: The Art of Doing Twice the Work in Half the Time*, illustrated ed., Currency, 2014.

[15] Peter Thiel, *Zero to One: Notes on Startups, or How to Build the Future*, illustrated ed., Currency, 2014.

[16] Chis Voss, *Never Split the Difference: Negotiating as if Your Life Depended on It*, 1st ed., Harper Business, 2016.

Index

Acknowledgments

Writing these pages has been a journey of a lifetime. I can't thank the amazing people enough who, one way or another, have shared part of this path with me. Their friendship, support, criticism, and generosity with their time have helped me to sharpen the concepts of *The 4 Streams of Leadership*. I'm grateful to each and every one of them.

To Dave Myers, for the invaluable advice, conversations, and feedback that helped me countless times. To Michael Noonan, for listening attentively and challenging me to think and see things more clearly. To Caroline McCaffery, for the many discussions about professional development and for guiding me through hard problems.

To Matt Zeiler, for inviting me to walk alongside you for a while at Clarifai, an experience that taught me so much. To Joshua Tepper, for article reviews and for building products with unwavering enthusiasm. To Mike Conover, for working with me to build awesome teams and products. To Alex Kirtland, for the many conversations and brainstorms that fueled creativity.

To Michael Frank Martin, for reading the manuscript and debating ideas with rigor. To Aaron LaBerge, for the transformative work we did together, revolutionizing apps and pushing boundaries. To Brian Wheeler, for reviewing the manuscript and giving valuable feedback. To Vasu Kulkarni, for the thoughtful feedback on ideas and product development.

To Michael and Andrew Katz, for helping me learn a great deal at mParticle. To Jason Lynn, for the long debates of ideas that sparked new perspectives. To Pablo Calamera, for the career advice and for being generous with your time. To Max Clark, for being a perennial and contagious optimist.

To Nena Madonia Oshman, for seeing the potential of the book and working with me with dedication and optimism. To Michael Campbell, for believing in the potential of the book and guiding me to perfect all the details to publish it. To Mark Malatesta, for your instrumental help in writing the proposal and moving this book forward. To Carol Reed, for the early copyediting work and suggestions for better writing. To Conni Francini, for reviewing the book and getting the words right.

To Eduardo Cerqueira, Sergio Xavier, and Marcos Luna, for great conversations about nothing and everything. To Amadeo Romaguera, for early career advice and mentoring that lasted for many years.

To Wendy Grounds, Bill Yates, Kim Baillie, Fulyana Orsborn, and Anthony Fasano, for the insightful interviews shared with an audience of wonderful listeners, which brought depth and real-world resonance to these pages.

Finally, to my family: Adam, Bianca, Renata, May, and Edmo, for bringing meaning and fulfillment to my life.

Thank you all for your time, energy, and belief in this project. This book is better because of you.

About the Author

Dalmo Cirne is a professional with three decades of experience in leadership, management, and technology. He has a degree in mathematics from SUNY (State University of New York) and is passionate about building products and enabling the next generation of leaders and individual contributors. He holds patents in software engineering and machine learning, fields he has worked on at startups and large corporations.

Throughout his career, Dalmo has seen the world changing at a fast pace and realized that just teaching what is already known is an insufficient condition for success. Knowledge itself has to evolve, adapt to new realities, and sometimes influence what things will become. He identified the need for an evolutionary type of leader who would base results on realistic objective criteria.

What is different about his work is that it presents explanatory knowledge for *why*, *what*, *when*, and *how* to go about the topics he explores. In addition to content, whenever possible, he includes complementary real-life examples to illustrate the principles in practice.

At Workday, his teams build the machine learning-based financial products; at Clarifai, computer vision was brought to mobile and IoT devices used from apps to the defense of our skies; at mParticle, he was part of taking the company from zero to one and establish the CDP market; at Disney, video and notifications enabled a whole new way to experience sports.